Jury Party

TAKING RESPONSIBLE CHARGE
OF OUR GOVERNMENT

S. Roy Johnson

JuryParty.org

Published by JURYPARTY.ORG

Jury Party/S. Roy Johnson—1st ed.
ISBN-13: 978-0-6924237-1-4 (JURYPARTY.ORG)

Contact:
S. Roy Johnson
JURYPARTY.ORG
AUTHOR@JURYPARTY.ORG

Editing by WordsArt
DLAMONT.COM

Book Layout ©2013 BookDesignTemplates.com

Contents

Contents iii

Introduction v

Chapter 1 — A New Way to Take Responsible Charge of Our Government 1

Chapter 2 — Aristocracy and Institutions 15

Chapter 3 — Where We Are Now: Our Existing System 33

Chapter 4 — Fundamental Problems with Republican Government 53

Chapter 5 — A Trusted System 85

Chapter 6 — Good Governance 95

Chapter 7 — Creating the Jury Party 107

Chapter 8 — Ideas and Suggestions for Implementing the Jury Party 151

Chapter 9 — The Opposition 199

Chapter 10 — Conclusion 221

About the Author 231

Notes 232

Introduction

A 2013 Gallup poll found that 60% of the American people believe that a third party is needed—a record high in the history of the poll. The poll also found that only 26% of the American people believe that the two parties are doing an adequate job—a record low.[1]

Perhaps this comment from UK journalist George Monbiot, from an article titled "Why Politics Fails," published at MONBIOT.COM on November 11, 2013, can enlighten us:

> So I don't blame people for giving up on politics.... When a state-corporate nexus of power has bypassed democracy and made a mockery of the voting process, when an unreformed political funding system ensures that parties can be bought and sold, when politicians [of the main parties] stand and watch as public services are divvied up by a grubby cabal of privateers, what is left of this system that inspires us to participate?[2]

Apparently England has just as bad a political system as we do. Some British view England's political party system with disdain equal to that with which we Americans view our own. It's not just our problem.

Special Interests Instead of Checks and Balances

Where are the checks and balances in America's political system today? Lobbyists and special interests write the legislation that the politicians vote for. Lawyers are hired by the two parties or special interests to create ways of avoiding the law. Statisticians and marketing firms are hired by politicians to create an edge that wins elections by pretending they are the voice of the people. Vast sums of money are transferred to the political parties in return for favorable legislation and laws. Special interest groups even write the legislation that our elected representatives do not bother to read—not even to verify what they are being told is really in the bills.

Not even the media can claim to be free of special interests. It is sensitive to its advertisers, viewers, and board members; it tells people what they want the people to hear from their own perspective—even though it is not always what the people need to hear. The truth about issues is glossed over or outright left out because it does not fit in with the purposes of political leaders and their supporters.

This book proposes the theory that the system of electoral representation as currently practiced in western democracies cannot and will not work long-term. It explains why this system, partly designed by our nation's founders, did not change government to the degree that we give it credit for—even as radical and forward-thinking as it was at the time. The political parties of our system have seen to that.

In spite of the need for a third party expressed by so many Americans, third parties have had very little support in recent elections. This book describes a new political party that is organized and works so differently from other parties that it may be able to finally break the barriers that have limited the progress of third parties for so long. Based on randomly selected juries and representatives, it is dedicated to a true democracy and provides a practical way for the people to control their government.

Challenge to Change

So, if you read this book and agree with me that random representation is the way to go, then what? The Republicans and Democrats will never let it happen inside their parties. Can you imagine either party saying: "Sounds great, we'll close our doors to the power players in the country—and their money"? Ain't gonna happen. Most mainstream party loyalists will probably dismiss the concept immediately because it doesn't fit their concept of how things should be run in America.

Any efforts at random representation will have to be grassroots, bottom-up, populist movements resulting in a groundswell of overwhelming popular support for the Jury Party. This can happen little by little with proven success stories used to sell and promote the concept to mainstream America, resulting in getting Jury Party representatives elected.

This movement can start by making small gains, promoting its successes, knocking a few incumbents out of office and succeeding locally. It can be a real voice for the people and a powerful go-between with government agencies, politicians and voters, until one day, in one election, this new system takes everybody by surprise and knocks either of the two parties out of majority party status and becomes a strong third party that stuns the special interests and party bosses. This movement can convince mainstream America that a jury type system is the way to go—a system that actually solves problems that government can't or won't fix. Initially, from small groups that make strong inroads in certain regions of the country, the party will affect some elections or legislative outcomes. The small groups will be working to build a reputation for success, spreading the word to family, friends, coworkers and neighbors while gaining the confidence that the American people actually do have what it takes to rule their land.

We will have to start the party at the bottom and work our way up, using a tier system. This means that the structure will grow from one party level to the next using random selection and fair voting methods to ensure that honest and high-quality people advance to the level of selecting our representatives. And we are not talking about just our representatives here. No, we are talking about the entire federal, state and local government system. Every agency must be governed by the people via a jury-based system, no exceptions. Every bureaucracy must be subject to the people's oversight and be under the people's "responsible charge." The people must restore and *become* the checks and balances of the government. The morals and ethics of the American people must be represented in all government agencies as well as in the laws of the land. We, as a people, can no longer just vote, sit and watch as our country goes down the wrong path.

If this or a similar democratic-based system takes hold of our country, then the people will govern their own land. Imagine discovering that your U.S. Senator lied about his support on an issue due to his ties to a special interest. You go in front of a jury and state your case, resulting in an investigation confirming your statements that initiates the recall process. This results in the removal of the Senator from his duties, all in just a few months. That's real power to the people that will get the corruption and special interests out of Washington, our state capitals and local governments.

How This Book is Organized

Chapter 1, "A New Way to Take Responsible Charge of Our Government," discusses the failings of the current two-party system, people's dissatisfaction with it, and the concept of a new political party and system based on broad participation of the people via randomly selected juries.

Chapter 2, "Aristocracy and Institutions," reviews a little history to see how we got to where we are today.

Chapter 3, "Where We Are Now: Our Existing System," looks at our existing system and how this system inhibits good governance.

Chapter 4, "Fundamental Problems with Republican Government," looks at the systemic problems that I see as the greatest roadblocks to the people's participation in government. That is, after all, what is needed: the people participating in government.

Chapter 5, "A Trusted System," theorizes about the possibility of existing in a truly trusted system, a system of governance that is inherently trustworthy.

Chapter 6, "Good Governance," reviews the concepts of good governance and the important roles that all people play in the execution of good governance. This section looks closely at the development of ideas from outside the mainstream and looks at how to get these ideas developed and implemented quickly.

Chapter 7, "Creating the Jury Party," describes the steps of creating and running a local organization based on random representation and taking responsible charge of our elected representatives.

Chapter 8, "Ideas and Suggestions for Implementing the Jury Party," reviews and comments on the structural and participatory requirements of the processes described in chapter 7.

Chapter 9, "The Opposition," reviews the potential opposition to this party, which may be great. But there are many strengths that the opposition will have extreme difficulty overcoming.

Chapter 10. "Conclusion" summarizes the arguments presented in this book and makes a plea to the American people to take responsible charge of their country to ensure the safety and freedoms of future generations. Includes a proposed Mission Statement for the Jury Party.

The numbered notes found throughout lead to full references of the publications and websites used in the book in the "Notes" section at the end.

The concepts proposed in this book comprise a first step at a new way of looking at the role of government and the relationship of government with the governed. The theories and practices for this party will be refined and improved upon as larger numbers of people become members and provide the feedback required for improvement of the organization. Practice makes perfect and there is no doubt that an ample number of Americans can perfect the initial concepts proposed within these pages.

Chapter 1 — A New Way to Take Responsible Charge of Our Government

There is nothing which I dread so much as a division of the republic into two great parties, each arranged under its leader, and concerting measures in opposition to each other. This, in my humble apprehension, is to be dreaded as the greatest political evil under our Constitution. —*JOHN ADAMS, 2nd U.S. President*

Politics and the Two-Party System

Let's take a look at the existing political parties in the U.S. Aside from the two large main parties, the Democrats and the Republicans, as of this writing there are thirty-one smaller parties, commonly referred to as "third parties." And *Wikipedia* reports that there were forty-five other parties formed at some time in our nation's history which no longer exist.[3]

Per the Gallup Poll of January 2014, 29 percent of American voters consider themselves Democrat, 24 percent Republican and 42 percent Independent.[4]

In other words, almost half of all voters are independent of the two major parties, probably because they disagree with the agendas of both parties sufficiently to remain unattached. According to ELECTPROJECT.ORG there were less than 82 out of 227 million votes cast in the 2014 election.[5] Or about 145 million eligible voters did not vote (approximately 50 million more than 2012). Why not? Are Americans disengaged with the political system because they are not involved in the day-to-day running of their government and/or because they feel that the rigid two-party philosophical structure effectively excludes them from participation?

All the existing parties have one thing in common: if you do not follow their philosophical dictates and leanings, you won't get very far in the party with your ideas. There were ten third-party candidates running for president in the 2012 election in Florida. Let's take a look at some of the third-party alternatives to the two-party system and their basic philosophies:

- ***OBJ - The Objectivist Party***—dedicated to Ayn Rand. If you believe in Ayn Rand's philosophy, then this is your place; if not, they will not listen to you, will they?
- ***LBT - The Libertarian Party***—dedicated to minimum government and a live-and-let-live philosophy. If you think government should play a larger role, then this is not your place.
- ***CPF - The Constitution Party of Florida***—if you agree with "their" interpretation of the Constitution, you should be able to fit right in.
- ***GRE - The Green Party***—if all you care about is environmentalism, then this party is for you.

- ***REF - The Reform Party***—opposes the two-party system and desires sensible and responsible government; Formed by Ross Perot in 1995.
- ***SOC - The Socialist Party***—if you don't like socialism; you won't like their world at all.
- ***PSL - The Party for Socialism and Liberation***—another socialist party.
- ***PFP - The Peace and Freedom Party***—another socialist party that also believes in ecology, feminism—and democracy! So, if the majority of party members democratically decided against socialism, ecology or feminism, the party would supposedly change into something else or disappear.
- ***AIP - The American Independent Party***—a very far-right party. Liberals need to convert or keep quiet.
- ***JPF - The Justice Party***—pretty much a liberal wing of the Democratic Party. Believe or move on.

So we see that, for example, if you care about the environment and have simple ideas that could be implemented cost-effectively, don't bother joining the Republican Party. If you think the government should make an effort to be sure everyone has healthcare, don't join the Libertarian Party. If you think that government has encroached on our lives far too much, don't join the Democratic Party… and so forth.

How many times have we heard the phrase "throw the bums out"? And in the next election some of the bums are thrown out, but most remain and many of the new reps become tomorrow's bums. And it seems the bums are in both the Democratic and Republican parties, so how can we accomplish much more than elect new bums? It's the *system* that needs fixing, not the politicians. You, the American people, can fix the system without the help of the media, government or even the politicians themselves.

A New Way to Get Things Done

The Jury Party will be a community-based, participatory system that can easily reflect the will of the people without compromising minority rights (and each of us, at one time or another, is a member of a minority). The actual goal is to create a *system of governance* that resolves issues more quickly and more efficiently, is more responsive to the needs of the people, more cost-effective, and is more reflective of the values and ethics of the people. It will allow the development of creative solutions and be as honest as the day is long—a new system that easily meshes and works with our existing Constitution and laws.

Public knowledge of the existence of the Jury Party may only require a few hundred thousand members nationwide. As of 2012, the Libertarian Party had 330,811 members and the Green Party had 250,682 members.[6] The number of people joining the Jury Party does not have to be all that high to have an impact, at least initially. Since the basis of the Jury Party is an active participation, the party may get far more attention than just that of registered voter or membership numbers. And the Jury Party does not require registration. You can keep your Republican or Democrat registration and still be a very active member in the Jury Party, and even be selected to run for public office. No one should be turned away for any reason.

No Agenda or Ideology

Any organization required by the people to provide the truth must be above influence or ideology. It must be self-supported and not be obsessed with power and influence, money and clout. Nor can this institution be led by powerful leaders who are obsessed with their own prestige and position in disregard of the value their institution provides, or is supposed to provide our country. There is only one such institution in this country that comes close to these characteristics—the jury.

The Jury Party has no agenda and no ideology except that the people should be able to participate in and take a part in determining the course of their local governments and that of the country. Therefore, anything goes. If a member of the Jury Party has good and economical ideas to improve the environment, then they can convince an economically oriented conservative audience that these should be implemented. Discussions are focused at *solving the problem,* not sticking with a philosophical agenda handed down by the powers above. Compromise will be essential in order to move forward, but an open discussion should also attract new ideas that resolve the issue satisfactorily for both sides in many cases.

Since this book does not go into detail beyond the effort of selecting and then working with an elected representative, this system will need to be developed further to eventually enter all aspects of government. This is all theory, of course, and it will take the time and passion of a great many people to bring this system to the forefront of our political system. I am not even going to pretend that I know how this will eventually pan out, but it can only be significantly beneficial to all the people when the members, with their vast knowledge and experience, passionately come together to form and operate these juries.

Random Selection and Greek Democracy

This new system will select at random a group of citizens to work together to solve local problems. All the local groups (which I call the first level or tier) will then select representatives to the succeeding next higher level of the Party to focus and consolidate the work done by the local groups. The process of studying issues and finding solutions continues with one or two higher levels all the way to the statehouse or the U.S. House of Representatives.

I developed this idea based on practices of the ancient Greeks and a few modern authors who have proposed similar theories. These modern authors wrote, however, from an academic perspective. This book applies a more practical approach and a "how-to" method, and is supported by a website for the use of the party members, at JURYPARTY.ORG. This system will result in a truly democratic party for any group of citizens who choose to use it and work hard to make it successful.

I was a bit surprised when I discovered that the ancient Greek democracies governed based on random representation (actually random selection from landowners). I had always heard from cynics that we could do better picking our representatives randomly from the phone book, but to think that the Greeks and other Mediterranean city-states actually did that, and were very successful, truly shocked me. It spurred me to think about and research the possibilities and ask: How can we use random representation effectively in our system today?

Think about this: The Greeks, with no pattern or previous similar system to go by that we know of, developed a democratic system of government, and it was based on random representation. They had no history of democratic principles that historians are aware of to base their theories on; this was original thinking that had to be developed from theory to application without past experience as a guide. Their instinct when they developed the concept of "people power" in government was to use random selection. There was more to it than just random selection, of course; a randomly selected candidate went through extensive interviews before actually taking office to be sure he was qualified for the position. And I'm sure the interviews were used to be certain that the interviewee agreed for the most part with the policies of the interviewers. People are people after all.

But this is the secret of the ancient Greek democracies that was not emphasized in school: *They chose random representation for their democracy*. Some of the reasons they did so may have been:

- To thin the herd of the outspoken agenda-drivers and their followers
- To prevent a small, connected minority from dominating the legislature
- To reduce or eliminate the power and effectiveness of the special interests
- To motivate those persons who typically would not run for office to do so through a sense of obligation

- To ensure that all people were represented in government
- To find representatives with no obligations and no debts to repay with their vote or support
- To force people of opposing views to talk to each other, unhampered by their philosophical divisions or the stubbornness of their leaders

This was the ancient Greeks' instinct as to how people should be governed. Is this mankind's instinct? And have our self-governing instincts been crushed by the culture of empire for the last two-thousand-plus years?

Ancient Greece had about 300,000 people, not 300 million as we do today in America. Obviously the Greek system of representation cannot work in America exactly as practiced by the ancient Greeks, but we can adapt their system to modern standards and demographics.

I would not expect good decisions from a Congress that was selected randomly from the phone book—not because they lacked honesty or an understanding of the issues, but because of their lack of experience. The government agencies and executive branch, due to their vast experience and system knowledge, would dominate legislators who did not have the skills to challenge such authority—skills that can require many years to obtain and execute effectively. Also, perhaps the Greek democracies could have survived to this day had they included all the people in the selection process, not just landowners.

Today we are having problems with agenda-drivers, small influential minorities, special interests, and poor choices of candidates for office from the two parties that dominate the political system. I believe all these problems can be eliminated with a representative system that uses some level of random selection to nominate political parties' candidates for office.

So how do we adapt these Greek theories and practices of democracy to the American Republic, a nation a thousand times the size of ancient Greece?

Basic Forms of Government

Before we continue, let us first look at the current basic forms of government that exist or have ever existed in the world. There are two very basic forms of government in the world today, republics and dictatorships. Dictatorships take several forms, from theocracies, monarchies, single political-party-led, and military governments to family dynasties or sole dictatorships. Republics also take several forms, such as constitutional or parliamentarian republics with varying degrees of authority between the executive, judicial and legislative branches. These republican forms of government are typically lumped together under the heading of democracies, although some are referred to as dictatorships if our government does not like the chosen victor or suspects election fraud.

The United States is a republic, not a democracy. The majority of countries in the world today are some form of a republic. In a republic, the people elect a body of representatives and/or one or more executive branch leaders with the vested power from the people to run things for them. But in the United States (and most other republics, I believe), this delegation of power from the people means that, in reality, the people are electing their *rulers*.

This assertion would be unpalatable to many Americans, for Americans traditionally believe that they have the say over their representatives, who should govern according to the people's wishes and permission. This tradition and practice is continually given lip-service by politicians and members of government, but largely ignored and/or outright fought as they carry on with their vested adherence to the special interests that truly guide their decisions. The system described in this book is designed to return this right to the people in fact and in practice—not just as lip-service.

A pure democracy, a country run solely by "people power," does not exist anywhere in the world today, to my knowledge. The term "democracy" has been hijacked to mean voting for your representatives, but that is not what the originators of the term meant. *The Greeks did not vote for rulers, they voted for policy.* In other words, they ran things *themselves* with the vote. And the only way to avoid having to vote for representatives to make decisions for you—a serious flaw in government according to the Greeks—was by using random representation.

Democracies can govern in several ways. First there is "mob" rule, which is what republican propagandists argue a democracy is. Second, a democracy can use the popular vote, like Switzerland, a republic with the democratic virtue of allowing the people to override legislation that is unpopular. Democratic principles in American politics allow the people to vote for amendments to their state constitutions. Then there is a third form of democracy, as promoted here—one where the people are in responsible charge of their government, with the responsibility of developing and deciding on policy. This proposal can be described as a "merging" of the government and the people.

You cannot take responsible charge of anything unless you are intimately familiar with the entity that you are in charge of. The following list of definitions of "responsible charge" have been borrowed from professional engineering definitions and adapted here to describe the qualities of a people necessary to govern themselves. The definitions are:

- "Responsible charge" may be defined as the degree of control a people are required to exercise over government policy made by elected officials or government administrators and operations.
- A people in responsible charge of their government should have the knowledge to discuss in detail the issues of the day or pending legislation.
- A people in responsible charge should be satisfied with the area of government they have authority over and should have authority to review and revise policy or pending legislation that falls into their area of expertise.
- A people in responsible charge should have first-hand knowledge of the skills required and an accurate assessment of the skills available inside the government entity they have authority over.
- The people in responsible charge should take full responsibility for their decisions and the operations of the government entity and, if found to be deficient, take the required measures to correct the decisions, or the flaws in the government entity, to obtain the desired goals.

In summary, you do not vote at all in dictatorships, you vote for your rulers in republics, and you develop and vote for *policy* or *laws* in democracies.

This book describes and justifies an organizational structure with the potential to obtain a democracy as described above, a system that puts the people in responsible charge of their government—a true and effective democracy. I hope you agree and find this book a good start on the road to a truly democratic nation.

Previous Works on Random Representation

There have been two books written on a version of random representation commonly called "demarchy": *Random Selection in Politics* by Lyn Carson and Brian Martin, published in 1999 by Praeger Publishers,[7] and *Is Democracy Possible?* by John Burnheim, published in 1985 by University of California Press.[8] In *Is Democracy Possible?* Burnheim does a good job explaining the faults of electoral representation systems and advocates random representation as a viable alternative. *Random Selection in Politics* also goes into the benefits of random selection of the electoral process.

Along with a few theories on direct democracy and some rare academic papers on the subject, that is about all I could find when I searched the internet for "random representation" or "government by jury" and researched the links and references.

What I got from the above two books was an academic analysis of the possibilities and justification for random representation. But all sources I found had a common thread: they believed that you need *government* to decide that random representation is the way to go. It is clear to me that that will never happen. *Government will never willingly give up its power to the people—not now, not ever.*

Standing out as one excellent exception to this scarcity of use of random selection is the Jefferson Center of Minneapolis, Minnesota.[9] The Jefferson Center is actually putting random selection into practical political use. It has organized numerous groups to study important issues. These have resulted in solutions that are forwarded to the government officials who authorized the studies.

Studying the Greek democracies taught me one thing. Before there were powerful agendas and special interests, before society got all complicated and economies were run by the economic "geniuses," the Greeks saw what fair and responsible government was. Real freedom was the community behaving responsibly and allowing all people (at that time, all who owned land) to play a part, or have a chance to play a part, in the running of government. There were no popularity contests, no slick ad campaigns, no special interest money, no negative campaigning—none of the things that disillusion Americans with the political process today.

Chapter 2 — Aristocracy and Institutions

> I am not an advocate for frequent changes in laws and constitutions, but laws and institutions must go hand in hand with the progress of the human mind. As that becomes more developed, more enlightened, as new discoveries are made, new truths discovered and manners and opinions change, with the change of circumstances, institutions must advance also to keep pace with the times. We might as well require a man to wear still the coat which fitted him when a boy as civilized society to remain ever under the regimen of their barbarous ancestors. —*THOMAS JEFFERSON MEMORIAL, Washington DC, Panel No. 4*

America's Aristocrats

Throughout history, mankind has endeavored to find tranquility in his system of government. Playing on people's insecurities has been a potent tool of governments, creating dictatorships, monarchies, fascist, communist and socialist governments that promise to take care of the problems that beset a people. Often these government leaders or theorists were sincere in their approach, although they ultimately determined that their system of government required ruthless enforcement to create a benevolent society—a contradiction in terms, as these stated motives have created some of the bloodiest regimes. Or, the rulers' character consisted of power-hungry greed, yet they were able to put forth a great sales pitch. They are history's aristocrats and ruling classes.

Our system of government today was devised over 200 years ago after the American colonies broke away from England. The founders of our nation created a government which ignored and dissolved the bloodlines that ruled much of Europe. They saw firsthand the corruption that resulted when religion and government ruled together. They separated the bloodlines and the church from the state for these reasons. But they did not separate the aristocracy from government. I am arguing that the personality and character that dominated the European churches, royal families, strong parliaments and their supporters and beneficiaries in the eighteenth century now dominate many of the institutions that control America including the two main political parties. These people simply moved to Wall Street, the corporate boardrooms, the union halls, government agencies, political parties, banks and well-funded foundations.

Aristocracy is defined today as "rule by the wealthy." In ancient Greece it was defined as "rule by the best." But can the "best" be the best rulers? Can the wealthy be the best rulers, no matter their conviction that they alone are entitled to rule? We do not place the "best" or "wealthiest" jurors on a jury to judge your guilt or innocence; rather, we place a random selection of ordinary people totally unfamiliar with your case to judge you. If it works in criminal and civil courts, why can't it work in formulating and executing government policy? If a random selection of people can judge the guilt or innocence of an accused murderer, then surely a random selection of people can justify the funding of a new interstate highway branch.

This country's founders were aristocrats, not always by virtue of their blood or a powerful position in a church, but through demonstrating personal excellence and commitment. They devised a system not where the people ruled, but where the self-made aristocracy ruled. The people were only given a choice of *which* aristocrats made the rules. In 1787 this was a radical and effective new system of government, but the result is that another aristocracy rules America today for its own benefit.

Ask yourself this question: Why is the Bill of Rights not part of the body of the Constitution? (These first ten amendments to the Constitution guarantee many personal freedoms, limit certain government powers, and reserve various powers to the states and the public.) The answer is that there was a group of founders (the Federalists) that did not want to give these rights to the people. This group wanted a strong federal government to rule America and dictate to the people the laws that the aristocracy wanted. They did not trust the people to rule their own land. They were aristocrats who felt that they, and only they, should make the rules that people live by. The Bill of Rights was brought into being to calm the fears of Anti-Federalists who had opposed ratifying the Constitution.

Are we being ruled by these same people today—not Federalists in name, but an aristocracy in fact? Do they dominate the upper ranks of both political parties?

All countries in the world are ruled by an aristocracy of some kind, so my question is this: If a people want to be free from all aristocracies, where are they to go? The answer is that there is no place to go that is free of all aristocracies. And if they could find a place that was free of a ruling aristocracy, would they not eventually create their own aristocracy? It's the *system* that needs changing—a system that naturally defends the people from their own self-created aristocracy.

A people must stand and fight for their rights against a powerful and stubborn aristocracy no matter what country they live in. Some aristocracies are worse than others and you might believe that America's is the best of the bunch. This may be true, but the aristocracy is never satisfied. They will find ways of taking all of your blood and treasure eventually unless you can create a ruling class that is no longer linked to an overindulgent aristocracy. You must be constantly vigilant and exert enormous energy if you are to maintain any level of freedom against a determined aristocracy today. Unfortunately, our system lacks the methods to do this effectively.

Yes, we vote for which of the aristocrats or aristocrats' puppets become our representatives, but we do not control those who control the representatives, nor do we control the agenda of the two dominant parties and their financial supporters. These aristocrats create a culture around their world, a world filled with other aristocrats creating policy and operating in an environment isolated from the American people. They influence each other, promote each other's interests, perform favors, influence laws and donate vast sums to elections and the two parties. This is done not in the interests of the people, but in the interests of the aristocracy and the institutions they run. Most representatives do not hear the people's words; they only hear the words of their fellow aristocrats.

Publicly, the issues are divisive, not uniting. There is nothing but conflict during an election—conflicts that confuse the voters over issues such as race, religion, culture, balanced budgets, foreign enemies, economic, liberal, conservative, Republican, Democrat, blue states, red states, etc., etc., etc. The aristocrats have deflected the people's attention away from solving problems and instead they are focused on conflict in an attempt to lull the people into a patriotic trance with a simple divide-and-conquer strategy.

America's Institutions

We work for an institution, we worship at an institution, we get our information from institutions, and we entrust our wealth, health, security and happiness to what these institutions provide us. The major political parties are institutions and what I am proposing here is a new institution. We rely on institutions to protect us, to give us answers that solve problems that promote the health and welfare of the people.

However, many of this nation's institutions are concerned with one thing and one thing only—increasing "the numbers." These institutions can easily be overtaken by special interests that only care about their own interests. The institution, whether it is government, charitable, educational, banking, religious or a corporation, must survive and grow at all costs. To not grow means failure of leadership. So the leaders of these institutions simply do not see the broader ramifications of what they are doing. Many are trained and programmed to only grow the numbers and nothing more. And the people have become the victims of these institutional agendas. The erosion of the middle class and/or national bankruptcy is inevitable.

So who is overseeing the institutions? Who, or what, provides us with knowledge that the institutions are doing what is right or formulating policy that promotes the general welfare? There is no institution that is inherently trustworthy, that the people can trust to give them the cold hard facts necessary to make good judgments and decisions. The answer is that *other* institutions are overseeing them. So we have to entrust some of these institutions with guarding us from the abuses that may occur from other institutions. The institutions oversee each other—or fail to do so, as the case may be. Isn't there something inherently wrong with this? Are the people who climb to the top of these institutions essentially similar in character?

The individual is largely overwhelmed and helpless against the institutions. For example, who argues that the Federal Reserve's monetary policy is the right long-term policy for America? Most of our representatives are not qualified to argue against the Federal Reserve Chairman. They have not spent decades studying the subject to the level necessary to argue for different policies with someone who has clearly done so and proven themselves in their career and publications. If our politicians are overwhelmed with the effort, then how can a typical American make a sound argument? We have to trust the selection process of the two political party institutions to oversee the institution of the Federal Reserve.

But what if a jury of the Chairman's peers were asking the tough questions? What if the jury was made up of self-taught laypersons and also a group of various academics from around the country, many of whom would qualify for the Federal Reserve Board as well? And what if these academics were each being guided and advised by a team of jurors in the preceding tier who were almost as qualified, if not equally so? Does this sound like a better way? In fact, would it not benefit the country if the Chairman was selected from this jury?

Despite my opinions about the dangers of the aristocracy running the country, this book absolutely does not advocate getting rid of the aristocracy and their institutions. The aristocracy consists of very energetic and often brilliant people and organizations who make great and often wonderful changes to our society. Some people think the aristocracy is the rich or "the best"—whatever that broad term really means—but I believe today's American aristocracy consists of the people who get things done. Often, they are the people with ideas who are able to get their agenda implemented, which results in success. Our relationship is mutually beneficial and must be allowed to prosper. Our society requires such people to be free to exercise their strengths in order for society and the nation to succeed. Because they are people who get things done, they typically gain wealth, power and influence through their efforts. Therefore, this book proposes that the aristocracy requires guidance and oversight from a well-organized and informed public with the authority to direct policy.

When institutions led by such people are left to their own morals and values, they might tend to fall off course; they become not the builders and movers in society, but the greedy of society. Because of this, they cannot be effective long-term rulers and deciders over the people. Even when people with good ideas are promoted to leadership, policy can fail because greed always follows on the coattails of good intentions. We can no longer trust the aristocracy with our blood and treasure; we can only trust ourselves. The *people* must provide the checks and balances for our institutions and their leaders—not the other government agencies or branches, and certainly not private institutions like the advertisement revenue-dependent mainstream media or privately financed political parties. The aristocracy cannot provide the checks and balances for itself. If the existing system continues, eventually all will be lost, because there is only so much a people can be pillaged before the foundation or core of the nation crumbles.

What are revolutions but just one aristocracy fighting another? Revolutionary success typically results in a worse government than the one it replaced. The people win little and often lose a great deal because revolutions are typically led by wannabe aristocrats, envious of the power and wealth of their established peers. We, the people, are simply fodder for each side, expendable tools to be used to overcome their opponents. These institutions often create their own culture, devoid of the big picture or reality. *Freedom should apply only to people, not institutions.* Institutions are machines that serve a purpose for the people. The people must be free to govern themselves, but institutions must never be free to dominate the decision-making process. We the people must become the rulers of the aristocracy in order to stop this behavior. We should not block them from their passions and endeavors, but we should provide the guidance and laws to ensure that their path and efforts match the goals—and do not harm the health and well-being—of the rest of the people, the nation and future generations.

Individual Qualifications

Does the ability of an individual who excels in one particular profession, such as law, politics, military, medicine, business or insurance, justify the individual's ability to rule over our lives, trespassing into fields he or she has little expertise in? Why is it that a successful lawyer should be permitted to make critical decisions about our education system, judge our environment needs, start wars, control our economic system, public safety system, engineering professions, medical system and so forth? Why do we give them, or any other profession, our trust to rule over us on issues most of its members have no expertise in? Perhaps they are more ambitious than others in this regard and thrust themselves into these roles with greater energy and the ability to work the system and obtain political funding. It is a very long-standing tradition in this country for members of certain professions and avocations (such as lawyers, members of wealthy families, and corporate leaders, to name a few) to enter politics and the public is used to this. Few citizens ever question it and their trust is automatic, when it should be granted deliberately and very carefully.

Aristocrats are not perfect. They have flaws just like all people and only excel in one or a very few characteristics that enable them to succeed. There is really very little difference between the top ten percent and the bottom ten percent in society. For those fortunate enough to have good character, positive family values, or wealth—or who experience lucky life-changing events that propel them into the aristocracy, their contribution can be great and we inhibit them at our own peril. But, they, like the rest of the population, have flaws—flaws that may even be exposed or amplified due to their success at obtaining excessive power and influence. Because of their success and position they may become intimidating, feel less challenged by others; their flaws are not given the boundaries that most people must live with. We therefore need a system of governing our institutions whose purpose is to allow the aristocracy to excel and the citizens to provide guidance in the institutions' direction; citizens should set the boundaries for institutions and the aristocrats who run them.

The real effort to find solutions is when experts in many fields come together to solve problems that involve many professions as well as common street knowledge. When all these people have a platform where they can express themselves and influence others to follow their point of view, then real solutions are possible.

For example, if business needs better-educated graduates, then they must talk with educators to describe the skills needed. Educators must talk to parents to address those needs and develop the methods required to succeed at the effort. Parents must ask how to inspire their children to make the effort and what is required of them for guidance. Taxpayers must talk to businesses to ask how this effort will be paid for and what the cost/benefit ratio is.

Another concern is when aristocrats battle each other for competing interests. Take the battle between industrialists and environmentalists, for example. These battles do not always result in doing the right thing; rather, the battle is fought and won to satisfy the interests or agenda of the aristocrats in both groups. Ordinary people, randomly selected, can be the jury for the conflicts of these two groups with the intent that we keep both employment and the environment healthy—isn't this the goal of all Americans? Alternate solutions that the two institutions cannot see within their areas of expertise can be explored to solve the concerns and interests of both institutions, instead of leaving it up to the lawyers and the courts, after the fact. This system of delayed judicial review only examines the issues from the narrowly defined viewpoints of the law, making irrelevant and unenforceable decisions likely that do not solve any real problems.

Here is a case in point, a true story. A big corporation bought up all the forest land in a county to supply wood for a new pulp mill. The people of the county had a long tradition of hunting in these woods. The bullets and shot embedded in the trees were causing a problem for the mill process and so the company banned hunting on the land. The hunters, made up mostly of WWII vets and local long-established families, raised a huge protest. The company backed off and proclaimed the land would always be available to the people of the county for hunting. The metal problem was engineered out with a simple low-cost solution.

If this happened today, the corporate managers would probably call their politicians, not their engineers. The entire county would be declared a hotbed of radical homegrown terrorism. Homeland security would be brought in and the media shrills would be given their marching orders to dehumanize the rebellion to the mainstream, install surveillance cameras or operate drones, and swat teams would be used to crush the uprising. People would be sent to expensive prisons. Tens of millions of dollars would be spent in order to save a hundred thousand. All this cost because the people involved were focused on winning instead of actually finding a simple solution to the problem.

Our current lifestyle and economy is squeezing us. There was the WWII generation that had a good life with just one income per family. Then dual household incomes offered many new opportunities to live a richer lifestyle. Now our lifestyle requires two incomes just to get by. Child labor laws restrict children from working, so the way the system extracts wealth from children is to get them saddled with college debt. What's next? Are we to work nights and weekends at a second or third job? Relax child labor laws? The elite are squeezing and manipulating the middle class into debt servitude. Yes, it is the people's fault for falling for it, but peer pressure and keeping up with the Joneses has been pushed onto our culture. If the system allows the aristocracy and our institutions to manipulate and fool the people by exploiting their cultural weaknesses, then the foundations of our country will eventually collapse. Our culture, like any culture, has strengths and weaknesses. All aristocracies will use the culture's strengths for their own gain and exploitation, sometimes for the common good. But the aristocracy will also use the culture's weaknesses for more profit. Only the people can place the checks and balances to defend themselves from this onslaught by very highly educated and well-trained aristocrats and their supporters. Sometimes the people will miss the assault, but sooner or later, they realize what has happened and, if the system permits, stop the assault in its tracks.

Our incomes are not keeping up with the cost of living, nor are they likely to in the near future. It takes great leaps in technology, radical central policy changes or the discovery of rich natural resources to significantly advance people's standard of living. This century will test us in our ability to use dwindling natural resources to maintain our quality of life since there may not be any great advances (comparable to the Industrial Revolution of the late 18th to mid-19th centuries) for a few generations to come. We, the people, must not let our government and their sponsors push us to the brink by ignoring the obvious. The community must be free and responsible to take charge of itself and its own security.

The people must take the next step in the evolution of government and free themselves from abuse in all its forms. The system presented in this book is only a small beginning and can be summarized as essentially expanding and empowering the jury process to oversee every aspect of government.

The Jury System

The jury system was institutionalized 800 years ago with the Magna Carta in England. Its roots go back to ancient Germanic tribal law and, as mentioned previously in Chapter 1, even Greek law as early as 500 BC. Its early roots more reflected a Grand Jury than today's typical trial jury, in that the jurors actually did the investigations themselves and then reported their findings to the courts, where they were verified and debated. The jury was instituted in response to a corrupt English king who convicted people he viewed as threatening. The land barons rebelled and forced the king to accept the jury system throughout the country. It worked. Very few people would ever consider abandoning the jury system, yet to this day it has not been expanded into other government functions.

If we do not trust our local police, judges and the district attorney (our neighbors), then why do we trust our elected officials and bureaucrats who are far removed from us? Government has expanded well beyond crime and punishment and into virtually every aspect of our lives since the Magna Carta was written; the jury system needs to expand as well in order to provide checks on all government activities. We can no longer trust the government to provide checks and balances on its own.

Isn't it better to form groups that focus on a single issue and thoroughly delve into the intricacies and details of the conflict or problem? Then, when a conclusion is reached, they advise or direct their representatives how to vote. Some people think this function already exists as carried out by bureaucracies, think tanks, special interest groups, lobbyists, etc. But remember, these groups seldom, if ever, reflect the wishes and needs of the American people at large. They are out for themselves or their clients' agenda. You, the American people, are not represented. You are just polled to see which aristocrat will win the argument.

As a side note, juries are able to declare a person innocent even if the person was caught red-handed. During the buildup to this nation's revolution, smugglers were routinely let go by juries because the people who made up the juries were tired of the British restrictions and taxes on the goods produced in the colonies. This is called jury nullification. This is when a jury returns a verdict of "not guilty" not because the state did not make its case, but because the jury felt the law was unfair, or poorly applied. It got so bad in the colonies that the British banned juries. Most judges rarely tell a jury that they have such power. If they did or it became widely known, I think many nonviolent criminal laws would be severely curtailed.

A jury system can be used in all branches and divisions of government to ensure that government policy, whether by elected officials or government bureaucrats, follows the will of the people and clearly reflects the people's moral and ethical values. If I am to be ruled, I wish to be ruled by a jury of my peers. My peers, like me, are not perfect, but I trust my peers more than I trust the elite and their hidden agendas and professional bias. I want to be ruled by people just like me, because they must live under the same rules that I do.

Most people have jobs that they perform well. If they are promoted into a higher position due to their qualifications and/or experience, they will eventually fit well into that position given a reasonable period of adjustment because their morals and ethics will drive them to perform to expectations. This is why juries succeed. And this is why the Jury Party can succeed.

But if a power- or prestige-hungry individual exploits her position by "kissing up" to the boss, if she degrades her fellow workers by exposing each and every mistake made and extolling her own undeserved successes, then she has a chance to gain a position of authority that she knows is undeserved. What characteristics would such a person portray in her new level of authority? Probably not good ones. If someone does nothing but strive for the next promotion by subterfuge or by requiring his underlings to do his work, what is he really good for? Isn't this the characteristic of many elected politicians—promoting their small success and degrading their opponent's minor flaws? In this book I show how the jury system removes such persons from the list of candidates. It will promote people who step up to the position they are given, where they can work until they are rotated out of office or no longer wish to continue their efforts.

In the Jury Party, a random group of citizens is selected who, after working together to solve local problems, select a representative to the succeeding level of the party and continue this process all the way to state government or the U.S. House of Representatives. Literally anyone who impresses the people he or she works with can make it to Congress. Is it better to vote for a stranger who is probably as incompetent, crooked or nuts as his opponents say he is, or to allow someone's peers, who worked closely with him for one or two years, to judge his character and qualifications for promotion?

The jury system proposed in this book has significantly more freedom and responsibility than the essentially passive judicial jury system. The jurors selected are essentially chairpersons of a committee with increasing authority from local, city and county to the state and federal levels. The members of the upper tier levels of the jury are selected through a combination of random selection and vote process. Other members of a group not selected on the jury have an equal voice to express themselves, but the jurors make the decisions and are the only ones selected by their fellow jurors to advance to the next tier or level.

We need a system that allows all people to be represented; the mainstream and the fringe idealists must sit around a table and discuss issues. This is our nature. It can be a source of truth that helps us make good and rational decisions. The existing forms of government today violate man's nature. They isolate and manipulate vast segments of the population, including huge majorities, through dictatorships and plutocracies. But everyone, from all segments of society, is needed to solve problems, discuss issues and provide the spark of ingenuity and invention that eventually forms effective policies. The mainstream is good at running things, but the fringe elements of our society act as canaries in the mine, warning the mainstream of catastrophe if their policies are not modified or changed.

Our current institutions of government, science, religion, education, agriculture and health isolate themselves and hold themselves above many other groups of people who should have a voice in society's path—to deny them that voice will invite failure.

Strengths and Weaknesses

There are many people in the country who have great ideas but no place to express these ideas or get the support they need to see these ideas through. They have no political ambitions and their ideas are probably in a rough format. Where can these people go to refine these great ideas in today's political system? Keep in mind that these people probably do not think that their ideas have much merit, or there may be something that they are missing in their hypothesis, or they have trouble selling their ideas to others because of their inability to express themselves effectively. There is no system in place that provides a path for expressing their ideas to the skilled and knowledgeable people who can provide the assistance they need. We all have weaknesses, so what we need is a system that pulls out and increases the strengths that each of us have and tempers or offsets our weaknesses.

This book promotes a jury based political party that will practice the jury processes of random selection and policy judgment before actually implementing this system into our government agencies. It will do this by nominating candidates for political office, each of whom will be both an important contributor and a subservient representative of the people's will. It will review and formulate policy and legislation that will benefit the country and its people. It will be a source of ideas that are promoted and implemented to the degree that is justifiably earned, not pushed through because of their image or profit. It will be a major challenge to convince the mainstream of the benefits of this system, but if successful, it could bring true democracy to all citizens. We now have new communication technology that provides a well-educated people with vast knowledge available at their fingertips; communication is fast, and information can be well organized, accurate and verifiable. Now, with these new tools, it is time, once again, to explore mankind's instincts of rule—it is time for random representation through the use of the jury system.

Chapter 3 — Where We Are Now: Our Existing System

Elites can manufacture consent because the average American is like a deaf spectator in the back row at a sporting event: He does not know what is happening, why it is happening, what ought to happen. —*WALTER LIPPMANN*

Although representative government has changed in the past couple of centuries, its characteristic feature of being a "democratic aristocracy" has remained. —*MANIN 1997*

When voting started, democracy ended. —*ANCIENT GREEK PHILOSOPHER, POSSIBLY ARISTOTLE*

None are more hopelessly enslaved than those who falsely believe they are free. —*JOHANN WOLFGANG VAN GOETHE*

We view ourselves as a democracy, but do we live in a democracy? Democracy is literally translated from Greek as "people power." Do the people have the power in the U.S.? We elect representatives who are supposed to represent their constituents' interests. But do they? Ask yourself if the people in America rule. If your answer is no, then we are certainly not a democracy in your view and if the majority of Americans hold this view, then our nation is most definitely not a democracy. And if people do not believe that the people have the power, then you cannot possibly call yourselves a free people. The elites that control the power determine the level of freedom the people will have and then propagandize how free we are. No power equals no freedom. It's that simple.

John Burnheim in his 1985 book, *Is Democracy Possible?*, wrote, "A democracy that renders the people impotent is no democracy."[10] Since the representatives we vote for are removed from the general populace and sent to state capitals or Washington to be influenced by lobbyists and party leaders, the people are removed from the political process. We have become impotent, and therefore, we are not a democracy. The only connection the people have to their government is the elections, which are controlled by party favorites, supporters, financiers and power brokers. The people in America are rendered impotent except in highly publicized issues which in some cases are not generally that important to formulating government policy.

If the people are impotent, then the special interests are empowered. Special interests can be defined as money, support or voter blocks given to elected officials or their political party in various forms from individuals and organizations which want, and expect, something in return. Unlike common people who donate unconditionally to support a candidate or party that they feel best represents their interest, special interests are the rich, influential and powerful, who are investing in an agenda. They expect a return on that investment and that return generally is not in the best interest of the American people, but only their own interest or that of their philosophical bent. If the special interests actually do control Washington, then we have taxation without representation and a total disregard for the American people by our two political parties.

Think clearly here: these special interest groups are constantly working on your representative. They completely dominate the Washington scene and many state capitals as well, like the American Legislative Exchange Council does (ALEC, discussed in the next chapter). Your representative and the political party bosses are in constant contact with these groups, not you. You are on their radar for only one day every two years and they have an army of well-trained campaign staffers and party experts, paid for by the special interest donations to take care of that little nuisance known as the American public. The lobbyists and special interests swarm all over Washington and state capitals. They would not be there if they were not wildly successful at what they have accomplished. The system is obviously designed for them to succeed.

The advantage with the Jury Party is that the money game disappears. And today, money seems to be the major culprit, by far, of poor governance, as described by countless books and articles on corporate influence, campaign donations, tax policy, military spending, bureaucratic regulations and foreign policy. Also, the money seems to be very effective at permitting the cover-up of any mistakes, so the errors fester for decades, making expensive boondoggles out of what could have required only minor repairs. There is an old saying in the engineering business. Fixing a mistake in design costs a dollar; wait till the planning stage it will cost ten dollars, and during construction the mistake can be fixed for 100 dollars. After construction, the mistake can cost 1,000 dollars and up. The Jury Party will largely prevent the problem from getting out of the design or the planning stage, because all eyes and ears have a voice.

If our current system of government can be summed up critically, it may be in this way: The people elect representatives who hand down rules and laws from above that the people must live by. Only when the people are very upset do our representatives change their minds on legislation. And there are no rules governing the representatives other than the rules they voluntarily place on themselves. Do you actually think such a system can work for the good of the entire populace? The government is a monopoly whose goal is to become bigger and more powerful and is very defensive of its authority and wealth—that is what monopolies do. Government must be a monopoly, but the people running and directing the government do not have to be part of the monopoly as it is today. The American people can make the government monopoly work the way they want it to, efficient and effective, if the people are willing to accept responsibility and work for the decisions that direct government policy.

Congress may not be made up of a good cross-section of the American people. After all, the Republican and Democrat parties are private institutions that are greatly influenced by financial donors and leaders with significant followings such as those found in environmental groups, business, labor, religious institutions, etc. The two dominant parties will not easily allow people to be elected without the support of these special interest elites because if one party abandoned these elites, the other party would dominate the elections. Therefore, it's obvious that the Democrat and Republican parties represent the elitists, not the people. We need a new party that represents the people only.

The Media

Can we trust the media to inform us of the information we need to make the right decisions on Election Day? The media is typically paid by some of these same special interests. Look at the national evening news programs. Virtually all of the commercials are selling drugs. Do you think the news media will tell the truth about the health-care bill if the consequence is a loss of income? The media is in business to make money, and that is *all* they are in business to do. If they cannot make money by telling the truth, they won't. If they cannot make money by performing in-depth investigations into government corruption and influence peddling, they won't do it. And in addition, it seems that many Americans are unconcerned with government corruption. The people believe the system will take care of itself or that there is nothing they can do about it.

Without the media reporting what is really happening in Washington and pushing for reform or criminal investigations, the people are really on their own with a general ignorance of the knowledge required in selecting our representatives. Our supposed watchdogs—at least as far as the national media is concerned, whose freedoms are singled out and guaranteed by the Constitution—may not be as effective as the people think they are.

It seems the mainstream media's goal is to narrow down liberal and conservative beliefs so they fit within very limited and fixed parameters. They wish to create very narrow-minded die-hard Republican and Democrat voters who will always be loyal at the polls. This way, victory is assured by the two parties. No third party can ever compete against the two narrowly defined parties with their die-hard legions of voters.

But they underestimate the American people; there are around 35% who are still thinking for themselves to some degree. They constitute a large minority which is desperately looking for a viable alternative to the status quo. We the people can only find such an alternative ourselves through a party that has only one ideological belief—the control of the government by the people. Once the Jury Party proves its integrity and effectiveness, the rest of America will soon follow.

One Messiah Please

Real political change will not come from the White House. Many people tend to have the messiah complex that believes real change will come from electing a president who will miraculously transform our federal government into a benevolent and wise system of governance. Somehow, a president, through sheer willpower, will transform the federal government from an institution that caters to special interests to an institution that caters to the interests of the people.

Such a political messiah doesn't exist. He or she is a figment of our collective imaginations, a product of historical monarchical traditions in almost every area of the world that has been passed down for centuries, both by still extant monarchies and by storytellers—and now by Hollywood, as well as through religious idealism and political hype. Hollywood typically promotes these beliefs in their historical dramas, cartoons and children's fare—for example, "The Lion King." Thus this messiah complex comes, at least in part, from these ancestral roots, typically the family monarchies and dictatorships of Europe, Asia and Africa. We are still looking for that individual, the "chosen one," if you will, who will lead us to victory. But though these are strong traditions, this is not our deepest nature; rather, it is our fantasy, resorted to partly in desperation and partly because we know no other way.

Even some of our Founding Fathers saw monarchy as a viable form of government. Here is a quote from John Adams, our second President, in a letter to Benjamin Rush in 1790:

> No nation under Heaven ever was, now is, nor ever will be qualified for a Republican Government, unless you mean ... resulting from a Balance of three powers, the Monarchical, Aristocratical, and Democratical ... Americans are particularly unfit for any Republic but the Aristo-Democratical Monarchy.

Frank Prochaska writes in his 2007 article "The American Monarchy," published in *History Today*:[11]

> The constitutional system adopted in the United States, with its ideal of checks and balances, was a creative modification of classical republican ideas suited to American social realities. But when those checks and balances do not operate effectively—as happens from time to time in American history—the powers of the presidency are arguably more akin to those of an absolute monarch like Charles I than to those of a limited monarch like George III. The

> effective American propaganda campaign skewed American perceptions of the great ironies of the US constitution that the Founding Fathers invested more power in the presidency than George III exercised as King.

In the same article Prochaska also wrote:

> Article 2 of the Constitution gave the President the more significant and problematic title, Commander in Chief, which had longstanding royal associations, having first been used by Charles I.

And this:

> In 1787, (Benjamin) Franklin, with philosophical detachment, observed in the Constitutional Convention: "It will be said that we do not propose to establish kings. I know it. But there is a natural inclination in mankind to Kingly Government. It sometimes relieves them from Aristocratic domination. They had rather have one tyrant than five hundred. It gives more of the appearance of equality among Citizens, and that they like."

And this gem about Alexander Hamilton:

> Hamilton wrote in his notes in 1787 that republics suffered from corruption and intrigue, while monarchical power provided vigorous execution of the laws and acted as a check on the other branches of government. "The Monarch must have proportional strength. He ought to be hereditary, and to have so

> much power, that it will not be his interest to risk much to acquire more."

Well, that says it all, doesn't it? Many of our founders were loyal subjects of Britain and King George before the Revolution. They respected hereditary monarchy and based the powers of the President on the current trends in Europe and Britain at that time.

Has the messiah or monarchical complex corrupted our political system? Have we reverted back to near absolute monarchy? Read this question from Jim Lehrer in the first presidential debate of 2008.

> Are you—are you willing to acknowledge both of you that this financial crisis is going to affect the way you *rule* the country as President of the United States.... [italic emphasis added]

Since when does the President "rule the country"? Are we electing a king for four years? The president is the leader/administrator of one-third of our government; he rules little. His actions must be in line with most of the cabinet and top government officials, then they must be approved by Congress and pass, if challenged, a constitutionality test through the court system. "Rule" does not apply to the position. There has been no mention of this in the media or by our leaders as far as I can find, which is a bit shocking and alarming to me. It's as if all this has been accepted by the people. In fact, you could argue that about 50 million voters prefer monarchy since that is the approximate voter turnout difference between a presidential election and a mid-term election.

The success or failure of mankind should never rest in the hands of *a* man, but in the hands *of* man. Our nature is to talk to each other and work together for our common goals. We do it every day at our workplace, school, places of worship and community organizations. What is needed in government is not the all-knowing, all-seeing, wise and generous messiah myth. What is needed is the all-involved, informed thoughts and energized will of the American people who will use their common sense and good character, powered by their passions, to create a truly free and incorruptible society—a society with leaders who are quickly replaced after poor performance or who lack the moral fiber of the represented. Our society is dependent on you, not a messiah—so get over it and get busy making a society you can be proud of!

If Only My Party Ruled

Some people believe they need to elect representatives who truly represent the people. They believe that if Congress or state legislators truly represented the people, then governance of the people, by the people and for the people would ensue. Many people are party loyalists who believe that their party will bring about prosperity and good governance, "if only we can get the other guys out of office."

The Republicans and Democrats have different agendas in public, but privately they are not so different. The Democrats took control of the White House in 2008 and had control of both houses. Have things really changed? The bailouts continued. Free spending continued. The housing collapse continued. The wars and threatening rhetoric continued. Nothing has really changed. A few liberal ideas have gotten through but no real change has occurred because the type of leadership remains the same and both parties have the same high-dollar supporters (in other words, investors). Even if you think the quality has improved in the White House, that leaves 99+% of the existing government still in place. And remember, the president was selected by his party and the party supporters because he agreed to their agenda. Do you actually think that the *real* party agenda is clearly spelled out in the party platform? No, so the U.S. President can't make that significant of a change to make a difference.

Each party has had the opportunity to dominate the government at one time or another and in each case they have been voted out of office by the people. This happened to the Democrats in the 2010 elections. The Republicans were booted out as well in 2006. The dominating party was unable to gain the trust of the American people simply because they did not know how, or had no intentions of providing good governance. The people, seemingly by defensive instinct, have tended to gravitate to a balanced two-party power system in recent decades.

At every election each party puts forth its agenda to get the vote out. They form strategies, not to solve problems, but to get elected. They come up with catchphrases that will get the people to vote for them, but after the election they join the system and are mainly concerned with consolidating power and getting re-elected. Is it even possible to have a competitive two-party system?

Let's go back to 1975 as an example. IBM and Digital Equipment Corporation were the two leading computer companies in America. Imagine that a law had been passed that declared these two companies were the only companies that could create new products in the computer and electronics industries for business and consumers. The creative minds of Apple, Intel, Amazon, Microsoft, Yahoo and Google would have had to be hired by these companies, prove themselves to their managers, get promoted, then sell their ideas to the management of these two companies—ideas that may have been quickly dismissed if the ideas did not fit the business plans of the company. These individuals would have had to climb way up the ladder of these companies before attaining the influence required to sell their ideas to the right people. Ask yourself if we would be anywhere close to the level of technology we have today if this had been the way it worked. A two-party system is no more a representative government than a two-corporation industry can be called capitalism. What our country needs is a surge of creativity in running governments. The combined, unique strengths of millions are far superior to the career ambitions of a few hundred. We just need a system that allows this to occur.

How many real solutions have you heard from candidates? The Republicans and Tea Party candidates intend to balance the budget. How? There is no place to cut except for the small safety-net programs that currently exist. They won't touch Medicare, Medicaid, Social Security, Defense or Homeland Security. There is really very little left. Essentially all the programs they can cut are the few things you actually get for your dollar, unless you're retired, sick or work in some way for the defense system or government. Education funding, the arts, national parks, OSHA, roads and bridges, regulators, environment, FDA and the Department of Agriculture inspectors are all available for the ax.

In other words, if you want to balance the budget, we must talk about tax hikes. Major tax hikes. But the needy interests will not allow this. The rich have their voices and the middle class theirs. Most government spending is on entitlements and defense, and the thought of reducing these budgets or raising taxes on the rich and middle class is political suicide—they won't do it. The people need an alternative path of expression and governance from what exists today in order to solve these problems.

Liberal vs. Conservative

Our country has been divided into two warring, stubborn, power-grabbing camps. Progress is impossible under these conditions. Every issue is replete with high drama that fills the news programs but bears few if any tangible results.

At the time of our independence, there were no liberal or conservative political parties, just Americans. We were divided by those who supported the Revolution and those who did not.

After the Revolution and before the Constitutional Convention, the political divisions began between the Federalists and the Anti-Federalists, later called the Democrat-Republicans. The Federalists wanted a strong federal government and the Anti-Federalists, led by Jefferson, wanted very limited government.

The Federalists won. In fact they control both of today's parties. Regardless of which party is in office, government size and influence increases. See the White House Office of Management and Budget historical budget numbers to verify.[12] And the problem with that is that the American people, or any nation's people for that matter, can only take so much government before the country cracks. Large and powerful governments create too great a burden on the people with taxes and costly regulations, and they comprise too great an attraction for the unscrupulous.

The community needs to organize and take responsibility for what the government does on a local level if it wants government to shrink to a sustainable size. Local means faster and more effective solutions for a lot lower cost.

Majority vs. Minority

We believe in majority rule with minority rights, but who says the majority knows what it is doing or is effectively expressing itself? Is the majority always right? Of course not, but where does the minority go to adequately express itself and convince the majority of its errors? When the majority has the power, they create major roadblocks for alternative ideas and policies. They create a power system that relies on the status quo. It takes years and mountains of evidence to reverse this status quo.

Culture

Do we have a cultural problem in America? I sense that the political and philosophical divisions of the two parties have created a different culture in America over the last forty years—a culture of "us" versus "them." Have they created a broad desire for instant gratification, a sense of entitlement, or a sense of uncompromising philosophical divide and dogma?

If we get involved in one of the two political parties we must first go with the flow. We are measured by our ability to help get people elected. With success, we are given influence and power to move the party in the direction we desire. Only very smart and energetic people can achieve this. They are very good at getting the influence through successful campaigns, but who says they are qualified at giving advice for the solutions to the problems of the country? They've never been tested for those criteria. They built their careers building image and then suddenly they are required to provide substance. Would we not be better served by someone who built their careers on substance alone? And built a team back home to support our representative that had a great image supported by great substance?

It seems that our culture is geared toward providing the base for launching successful careers. We invest heavily in county youth and school sports programs to support potential Olympians and professional athletes. We elevate people who have a gift for gab. People who are born with, or who have inherited or been raised on a sense of entitlement, are somehow elevated by our society; they are given enormous trust by the people and have tremendous initial confidence placed in them. Yet obviously, the American people are very disappointed by the results, based on surveys of the people's confidence in Congress, State governments, Wall Street, corporate America and particularly their primary news and information source—the mainstream media.

As pointed out by Laurence J. Peter and Raymond Hull in their 1969 book *The Peter Principle,*[13] do we promote good people until they reach their position of incompetence, which results in structural failures and short-sighted policies?

This is all speculation, but something seems to be fundamentally wrong with the way we select and promote leaders. Something is wrong with the amount of power we entrust in these people. Some people think we are led by greedy evil people. I don't think so. These are ordinary people with extreme skills and abilities who are victims of their success. They are people who clearly fit into our current system and when they experience repeated successes become entitled. They are entitled to more wealth and more power to create the systems that they believe in, and then dictate and enforce their opinions on us. That is essentially our system.

And when they are promoted due to their abilities, they are given power over things they are not expert in. They also can have philosophical blinders on, or be severely limited due to the system bureaucracy—the bureaucracy that protects the many mini-empires that feed off the American people.

It is my hope that the Jury Party promoted in this book will change the culture of how we control and govern our nation, government agencies and its public institutions—not by empowering a few "chosen ones," but by creating an organization that locates and promotes a wide variety of expertise and an easy path for innovation in all the areas that are needed for a successful community, state and nation.

Government often tries to pass legislation concerning culture or to rule through the judicial branch. When it does either of these things, there is always conflict and the changes made could simply change back and be much worse than before. The people must be the instigators of cultural change in society. This way, change is more acceptable and less likely to be challenged with force. But cultural conflict is inevitable unless people who yearn for change talk to the ones who like things the way they are. And in our culture, discussions between religions, races, ethnicity, generations and classes have no system in place to discuss their issues and form understandings and acceptance that would create a culture of tolerance of our differences.

The Jury Party forces these groups to talk to each other and provides the system used to implement the inevitable cultural changes. The Jury Party provides the meetings for these various groups to sit down with each other to discuss conflicts and come to understand each other's desires with a methodical system of change that eases into the community without much discord. Doesn't the judicial jury system do just that? A group of people with a wide variety of backgrounds must come together and agree, unanimously, on a given judgment.

Cultural conflict typically comes from a lack of knowledge. The only knowledge most of us have is how the other culture is affecting or going to affect our life. But we may be totally unaware of what our culture is doing to them! The Jury Party allows this knowledge to be shared, unlike in the current system of isolation, which uses control and law and exacerbates ignorance and fear.

Oligarchy

The United States' current system of leadership, whether in government or virtually any institution, still emulates the system of the old European monarchies and parliaments that ruled for over a thousand years. We still believe that a smaller, select group of elitists must make the decisions for the people and take care of the people. We either have been led to believe that this is the best system available, or do not know of an alternative system that can better help us express our views and successfully govern the country.

The American Revolution is, and always will be, revered as a defining moment for mankind away from the tyranny that ruled for so long. But what the American Revolution did was simply to remove the European royal bloodlines from the equation and institute laws to restrict monarchies or Parliaments from obtaining abusive power again. The result was that elitists could now come from all walks of life and from every class! This was a huge deal at the time, but today, relatively speaking, it's not such a great change; we are still ruled by elitists, many of whom do not deserve their status.

Wikipedia defines oligarchy as a system in which "power effectively rests with a small number of people".[14] Although the broad term "western representative government" is used to describe various countries' systems, some of them quite different from one another, many of them, including the United States, have moved away from representative government and are becoming oligarchies.

For example, Britain exerts very rigid control over its party members, forcing party representatives to follow the party line. Breaking from that line can have serious consequences, including expulsion. This sounds a lot like the forces controlling the Communist Party, which has strict rules against deviation from the party line. Unity reigns supreme.

You can see that "unity" of party members is the opposite of responsiveness to the electorate—the people. Unity demands adherence of policy and legislation to standards that party leaders dictate, not which the people wish or demand. Although many people from varying backgrounds are elected to office, to rise in stature and influence they must toe the line of the party. The successful ones are given positions of influence that allow them to channel Federal money to their local area and select constituents—often those who have lobbied them most effectively. But most of the electorate rarely become aware of just how unresponsive such elite representatives really are to their needs and desires or with whom their loyalties really lie. So people consider these representatives to be superior and continue to elect them, still being led to believe that they are responsive to the needs of the people through their reelection campaigns.

This system in fact promotes an oligarchy and the U.S. appears to have been moving into this type of system for many decades. In fact, it has operated this way to a greater or lesser extent, if covertly, during much of its history. The results of this system are the isolation and virtual disenfranchisement of vast segments of the population.

These ideas are reflected in a quote from Robert Michels appearing in *Wikipedia:*[15]

> Robert Michels believed that any political system eventually evolves into an oligarchy. He called this the *iron law of oligarchy*. According to this school of thought, modern democracies should be considered as oligarchies. In these systems, actual differences between viable political rivals are small, the oligarchic elite impose strict limits on what constitutes an acceptable and respectable political position, and politicians' careers depend heavily on unelected economic and media elites. Thus the popular phrase: there is only one political party, the incumbent party.

Yet these overbearing governments are totally dependent on the people they control. If the people do not go to work, then the government has no income, the wealth of the country is threatened and that motivates the elites to change their government to get people back to work. Almost all special interests that control governments today, regardless of the form they take, absolutely require the people to work for the preservation of their power and wealth.

Take the recent events in Egypt, for example. The people were not creating a violent confrontation, the government was. It was the government that emptied the prisons and let loose the criminals and government thugs onto the people, hoping to create a need for government protection. It didn't work. When the Egyptians began avoiding their jobs, the support for Mubarack quickly fell. With the system proposed in this book, the corrupt Egyptian police would have been fired a long time ago, their replacements would serve the people rather than the state, and law and order would have prevailed even during massive demonstrations. With police on the side of the people, the government has no way of enforcing its unfair dictates and its private armies will be challenged by the people and the police. A key to freedom is to get the police on the side of the people; a key to authoritarianism is to get the police on the side of the authorities.

Now it is time to finish the job and go back to that which the instinct of man calls for—away from the elitists' rule and back to leadership selected, at least to some degree, through random representation using the jury system.

Chapter 4 — Fundamental Problems with Republican Government

All tyranny needs to gain a foothold is for people of good conscience to remain silent. —*THOMAS JEFFERSON*

One is more certain to influence men, to produce more effect on them, by absurdities than by sensible ideas. —*NAPOLEON*

If liberty means anything at all, it means the right to tell people what they do not want to hear. —*GEORGE ORWELL*

I might have once been a liberal on some issues and a conservative on others, but I have abandoned that now. It is not the liberal agenda or the conservative agenda that is the solution to our problems; it's the system itself that needs to be changed. *The people need a system that puts the conflict on the table to be hammered out by all sides.* Once a compromised or creative solution is arrived at, it is then made into law by common citizens whose only agenda is to solve the problem. I don't care who gets their way anymore, just as long as their way is reviewed by a jury of citizens who have all the information necessary to make a rational decision, and who, if results do not meet expectations, can quickly modify or reverse the law before damage is done.

Below are the "systemic" problems of western style "democracies" run by political parties that I see as the major blocks to successful government.

The First Problem: We Don't Know Who We Are Electing

The first problem, which was a major driver of the system developed in this book, is that we really have no idea who we are electing to make the laws that we live under. Seriously, do you trust the people you are electing? Do you understand all the character traits that are required to drive an individual to want to be viewed as a leader in our current political environment, and are these character traits held in common with the American people or are they even beneficial to the country? Do you know who these people are, or do you just know what they want you to know? Are the images they portray "creations" designed by their campaign staff and party advisors? Campaigns have nothing to do with good governance. Campaigns get *electable* people elected, not necessarily the people who make good leaders or representatives. The object of this book is to change this system so the right people are selected to be the leaders and after they are elected their feet are held to the fire. The "fire" is the determination of the American people in their efforts to have a responsible, efficient and trusted government.

We have no confidence in our government because there is so much power in so few hands and so much political cost at stake with the party image and elections. They are playing a game of "not losing the next election" and not even risking a few seats in the House that could shift political power. The House and Senate leaders are mainly focused on getting or maintaining majority rule of their party due to the immense political clout that comes with being in the majority. This also has nothing to do with good governance.

If the people were properly informed and confident that the system that governs them was effective and as honest as humanly possible, then the political cost of decisions and the representative's "image" would become irrelevant since representatives would just be the voting member, not the decision maker of a participatory democracy. Good governance, monitored by a new participatory jury system, would take precedence over political competition and legislative stagnation.

The Second Problem: The System Discourages and Denies Public Participation

The second problem is how the system removes the people from participation. We go to polls to vote and then go home and criticize the results and complain for the next two years. When given an alternative at the next election, we are so influenced by massive negative campaigning and the fear of change that we generally continue to elect these same people back into office. People are not participating, so how can the people feel in charge and trust the judgments of their representatives? We can no longer permit ourselves to be lulled into a patriotic trance that allows politicians and their special interests to divide us philosophically and promote their own profit over the welfare of the American people. The methods presented in this book end this practice once and for all.

Consider the Occupy Wall Street movement. Will this movement be effective? Probably not. The media constantly criticizes the movement, points out and exaggerates every single flaw or problem, and just degrades the people involved in order to stop the movement and align the majority of people against it. The elected leaders have control of the police, who are simply obeying orders to push this embarrassment out of view. If the movement continues, then the powers that be will do something to appease many members into going home—and brutally respond to the ones who don't—a simple divide-and-conquer strategy. Whatever offerings were used to appease the protestors will simply be reversed later. That's how it's done. The system proposed in this book provides a platform for all people to express their concerns and present solutions to problems. No longer will the elected officials violate the constitutional rights of freedom of assembly and speech without the consent of the people. If the jury system or party were in place today, the Occupy Wall Street groups would not need public protest to express their concerns—just go to a Jury Party meeting and sell your ideas. Most protests will become a thing of the past.

It is hopeless to expect our current system to perform to the level that meets the people's expectations. The people do not want mistakes, excuses or other weaknesses, they just want zero problems, and an occasional righteous crusade doesn't hurt either. As a result, our leaders have learned to goose the system over the many decades of modern society. They have lived off the enormous wealth created by past generations.

Our system has become a formidable industry of lies and deception. You can't beat `em at their own game. Or can you?

What if we can create a political party that is unique in every way? Unique in the way it raises and spends campaign funds. Unique in the way it selects representatives. Unique in the way the people work with their representatives as participants in a democracy, not subjects in an oligarchy. Unique in how it controls its leaders and representatives.

The Third Problem: The System Doesn't Attract Good, Ethical People to Run for Office

For the third problem, consider this: Why would a person who has some good ideas of how to run the government; is in touch with the needs and abilities of people; could very well make government more effective; could create strong, long-term relationships with other countries; could prevent war; and would generally reflect the morals and ethics of the American people, run for high office? Why would a person of high moral character run a dirty, nasty, negative campaign against his or her opponent? Why would they go against everything they believe in and stand for, just to win an election? They wouldn't, of course, which is why they rarely run for office, and usually lose when they do. We mainly get the party power players who represent only a small influential minority of the general population and will say and promise anything to sell themselves to the rest. Is it any wonder that our legislatures are held in such low regard by the people today?

The Fourth Problem: Divisive Party Politics and Influence-Peddling Deceives the People

The fourth problem is party politics. Today, the United States is dominated by two private organizations called political parties, the Republicans and the Democrats. These two parties are in control of who will rule. Why should they rule? Where does it say in the Constitution that we are supposed to be ruled by two private, partisan organizations? It doesn't and it's time to get rid of this system, or at least reduce its influence. In fact, there were no political parties in existence when the Constitution was written. George Washington believed that political parties would divide the nation. John Adams' greatest fear was the two-party system. Were they right?

These two private organizations manage and direct our government. They appoint the top positions of agencies and departments and appoint the judges that legitimize the legality of the party's decisions. The problem is not government. The problem is the two private organizations that direct the operation of the government—the political parties.

Why do we call the process of selecting our rulers from a ferociously defended choice of two private organizations "freedom" and "democracy"? Because these two private organizations and their media shrills say it is, that's why. And we blindly follow like good little sheep.

Both parties have broken down into the liberal and conservative philosophies that divide this nation, just as predicted by Adams and Washington. Each philosophy can live separately or together in harmony, but only if they work toward this goal. The problem exists when one philosophy exerts its influence over the other and threatens its lifestyle or philosophical beliefs. This immediately creates conflict and division that fuels the next election with negative campaigning. What is needed in America is a system that helps these two philosophies, and the many more smaller beliefs, live in harmony and mutual understanding—a system that removes the emphasis on philosophical beliefs and *emphasizes practical answers regardless of the philosophy that may be associated with the solution.*

Unfortunately the party system has divided these two philosophies into warring camps. The purpose of this effort is to divert the people's attention away from the real problems in America—the problems the two parties do not want to, or cannot fix. This must end if we are to progress as a nation. We cannot succeed as a nation divided; that should be obvious. We must agree to disagree and work toward common ground and arrangements that leave both sides free to express their beliefs by leaving the other side alone with their beliefs. As long as the two-party system controls who runs the nation we will be a divided country; it must end.

The Fifth Problem: A Single Profession Dominates Government

The fifth problem is that one profession—the legal profession—has so thoroughly inserted itself into every function of each branch of government, that it exerts undue influence over all the actions and processes of government. Each time a piece of legislation is passed, an army of lawyers line up on each side to argue what the legislation really means. If we are electing such smart people, then why do they make so many obvious mistakes? Countless past leaders warned us in advance against the blunders that are nonetheless made every day now, yet our politicians relentlessly ignore the lessons of history.

Why are there so many lawyers in Congress? Lawyers dominate legislative bodies according to Dorothy Gambrell, in her 2013 article, "The 113th Congress, by the Numbers" published in *Business Week:* forty-five senators and 38% of the House comprised lawyers after the 2012 election.[16] When a single profession dominates the legislative and bureaucratic structure, it will naturally promote itself and create a "lawyer friendly" atmosphere throughout government and in society. Legislation has been passed that requires legal counsel on even mundane and simple issues. Whether it is wills, patents, real estate, minor business transactions, civil/criminal defense, etc., lawyers are almost always required. Only lawyers can even understand the legislation that we, the people must live under. We are forced to trust their judgments and put up with the costly legal battles each law brings forth. Because large companies have an army of lawyers that can dominate smaller, less resourceful businesses, they have a competitive advantage. Lawyers can clearly be extremely helpful to a truly people's government, but allowing one profession to dominate can only bring high costs and ineffective government that does not serve the people as well as it could. Lawyers should serve our elected leaders, not be our elected leaders—at least to the extent they are now.

Lawyers, or those in any other dominant profession, know best their own areas of expertise—not war, peace, education, commerce, agriculture, business, medicine, transportation, engineering, etc. So, if your representative is a lawyer or a doctor and has to decide how to vote on a farm bill, are you not allowing an amateur to make this decision? And how will he make this decision? Certainly not because he has first-hand knowledge. He will make the decision based on his party's position (defended by their creative and easily memorized one-liners) unless there is a substantial and expensive grass roots effort by the people in his district to vote otherwise.

Within the judicial system, a law firm "chooses sides" and comes up with the best arguments it can make to defend their clients and their positions. They are not held accountable for wrong arguments or failed cases and when they enter the legislative arena, they choose sides on legislation and are rarely held accountable for the poor or disastrous legislation they approve. The laws that are proven ineffective or wasteful remain on the books for many years until they are finally reversed when the people in power retire and a new generation of leaders takes over and modifies the laws that they are not beholden to.

These lawyers as legislators are making critical decisions on important issues such as global warming, not because they know they are right, but because they flipped a coin to choose a side instead of forcing science to come to a legitimate, honest, unbiased consensus. They do not know what is true any more than we do. Thus we have a 50/50 chance of being wrong here—a mistake that could be devastating to mankind or our economies.

The Sixth Problem: Special Interests Determine Laws and Government Actions

This brings me to the sixth problem. Legislators are overwhelmed by the mountains of knowledge required to make rational decisions about things they know nothing about. They cannot possibly have enough knowledge about all aspects of government and law to make the right decisions. So they must listen to their party leaders, who are taking orders from their party special interests, loyal voter blocks, or party gurus. Legislators, unless they are intimately knowledgeable about a bill before Congress, have no choice but to dish out the usual party line to their constituents in defense of their position.

The Affordable Care Act (Obamacare) was 2,500 pages long. How can anyone not intimately familiar with how the entire health-care system works possibly read, comprehend, research and argue such a massive piece of legislation? You need an army of dedicated experts to perform this task well enough to argue for or against such a bill. Our representatives have no choice but to toe the party line.

Clearly, most of our representatives are just following orders (not ours) on most legislation. So how can we conclude anything other than that representative government is a farce?

Now, imagine what goes on at the state level, where the legislators are paid far less, have much less time and substantially fewer staff to analyze and understand the legislation before them. No wonder an organization like the American Legislative Exchange Council (ALEC—discussed in problem number nine below) has such strong influence.

The Seventh Problem: Elected Reps Gain Power and Wealth at the Expense of the American People

The seventh problem consists of the fact that our elected representatives and bureaucratic organizations, in order to increase their power, influence and wealth, can only make gains through the extraction of power and wealth from the American people. Where else can they get it from? When they print money and raise debt they are literally extracting wealth from future generations to cover their unbalanced budgets. When bureaucracies want more control, bigger budgets and more responsibilities, they can only get this by removing control, money and responsibility from you. And if they continue to do this, year after year, decade after decade, Republican or Democrat, it is inevitable that the government (and its special interests) will one day have complete control of our lives and our treasure. Either you take control of your life and community, or the government and their sponsors will. And, if history proves anything, you will not like their rules one bit.

The Eighth Problem: The Influence of Powerful Institutions Is Greater Than That of the People

The eighth problem is the institution. As discussed in chapter 2, our society is institution-based. Institutions take on many forms. They are religions, think tanks, charities, universities, corporations, mafia organizations, research centers, local gangs, political parties, government and government agencies. Getting anything accomplished requires one of these, or a similar institution, to promote and/or approve the effort. These organizations are required in a functional society. The problem with these institutions is that there is little or no oversight by anything other than another institution. All these institutions have two things in common; (1) They must feed off the general population, directly or indirectly, and (2) They provide a path for power-hungry people to ascend to the aristocracy.

Institutions are, by nature, creators of the aristocracy. Institutions create levels of power for the power-seekers to ascend. Many institutions are self-serving and defensive of their influence, power, wealth and prestige. The leaders of institutions can never, by nature, ever come to the conclusion that the institution is no longer needed or has outlived its usefulness. Institutions must always find a reason for growth, whether deserved or not. An institution's leaders are driven to expand the institution because growth legitimizes and confirms the belief system of the institution, resulting in greater prestige for its leaders. Corporate executives are required to increase the numbers every year to appease their largest stockholders and Wall Street analysts. Planned obsolescence, a profit-making philosophy widely used by manufacturers in the twentieth century, was a good example of the institution extracting wealth from the people. The people had no clue what was happening because no institution was telling them so until very late in the era. Planned obsolescence can be devastating to the people working in an industry, such as what happened to the American automobile manufacturers when the Japanese car makers expanded their market share in the '70s, resulting in decades of depressed domestic jobs and a negative reputation.

The people who succeed in these institutions are the very people who promote the institution by improving the image, bringing in more money or increasing influence—in other words, the people who increase the stature or grow the numbers of the institution. Why were these people promoted within these institutions? Are they promoted because of hard work and good ideas? Sometimes, but often they are promoted because they fit the profile—the profile that best suits the institution for growing the numbers. The person that invented "planned obsolescence" was the kind of person that fits the profile. They are certainly not promoted for solving the problem that created the institution in the first place because that would result in its demise. That would be unthinkable for any institutional leader.

Often, the beginnings of these institutions were an honorable and worthy cause promoted by sincere people whose goals were to solve a problem, promote a charity, defend a group, build industries or make a fortune. These are all good and just causes that are required to create a successful society. Their successors, on the other hand, had to climb the ladder, get ahead and promote themselves by being an asset to the numbers and expanding the institution. Some do so honestly and some do not, and some do so without regard to the value that the institution actually provides, such as in the planned obsolescence example. These people have an insatiable need for power, income and prestige that strips them of morals or ethics they profess to have and demand from others. Their success takes precedence over the common everyday morals and ethics the people expect and take for granted from their peers and leaders.

Institutions will defend themselves from competition, criticism and threats to their prestige or power. They will attack any barriers to their goals, including, unfortunately, solutions or cost-effective alternatives to the institution's main focus. Many institutions use the government to promote their causes, defend their markets and attack their competition. Institutions and their leaders are essentially the special interests that control our government today; they comprise the American aristocracy. They find it much easier to sell their agenda to a few influential representatives than to the people at large.

The same types of people who defend, protect and promote institutions exist in our government as well. Hence, government and its departments can never shrink or reduce their budgets and authority over the people. Some bureaucrats get bonuses due to the number of employees they have in their department. If these managers solved problems and reduced the need and size of their department, then they would be punished with reduced bonuses. Can you imagine airport security ever going back to the levels before 9/11? Government leaders would never take the chance that there might be a terrorist attack the next day. But a jury of the people can. They are the ones standing in airport security lines and riding in the planes.

The corrupt leaders of these institutions are not severely punished by their fellow aristocrats. In other words, the good guys are not policing their own. Good cops look the other way when bad cops misbehave, good doctors look the other way when they have to fix the mistakes the bad doctors make, and good politicians look the other way when powerful politicians go wrong. Well, the good guys who keep silent are just as wrong as the bad guys. When will the good guys learn: the silence of the good guys is the strength of the bad guys? Just look at the plight of whistleblowers who have to go it alone. Why aren't whistleblowers getting support from all their "good guy" peers? Are the "good guys" that afraid or intimidated? If so, then we definitely need a different system.

So, if you're a Wall Street executive who needs favorable decisions by the Treasury Department, you and your peers will donate large sums to the political parties, who in turn promise to select your choice for a high position in the department after the election. It's that simple and perfectly legal. And with the recent Supreme Court decision in 2010 on corporate donations to campaigns and political parties, *Citizens United vs. Federal Election Commission,*[17] we are very likely to see increased erosion of the value of individual participation. The special interests' influence is about to go into overdrive. This five-to-four Supreme Court decision, brought forth by special interests who objected to the media's First Amendment freedom to promote their political candidates for office, continues the trend of distancing the American people from the election process. The court has determined that any institution can influence elections with unlimited funding and support, not just media institutions as guaranteed in the Constitution.

And just recently the U.S. Supreme Court has added a new dimension to the spending practices of the elite. On April 2, 2014, the Supreme Court ruled in *McCutcheon v. Federal Election Commission.*[18] The 2010 *Citizens United* decision had removed the limits on monetary campaign advocacy as long as it is independent of campaigns and the candidates. The *McCutcheon* decision retains the limits that individuals can give to candidates in a two-year election cycle ($2,600), but removes the total limits, allowing you now to give $2,600 each to an unlimited number of candidates. So what can a rich person do? Join a club of like-minded rich people and donate vast sums to all of the candidates of the political party that promotes their group's needs. In other words, find the candidates that fit the profile that these special interest groups require to get a large return on their investment. Maybe $2,600 won't make a difference to a congressional candidate, but $2.6 million will if the club has 1,000 wealthy donors or more.

Additionally, because of *Citizens United,* that same club can donate vast sums to negative advertising against the opposition party and positive advertising for the organizations that support their causes. The people have no defense against this onslaught because most people just do what they're told by the advertising or their favorite cable news talking head or just vote for the perceived lesser of two evils. Only the Jury Party and random selection can eliminate this from our system by developing solutions to problems regardless of outside biased advertising. Money needs to become worthless in politics if we are ever to have honesty in government. The financial requirements of the Jury Party are minimal compared to those of the established two parties.

Chief Justice Roberts' argument in the *McCutcheon* case includes the statement:

> An aggregate limit on how many candidates and committees an individual may support through contributions is not a modest restraint at all.[19]

And this:

> The government may no more restrict how many candidates or causes a donor may support than it may tell a newspaper how many candidates it may endorse.[20]

Good points maybe, but unfortunately this decision removes poorly designed limits without replacing them with well-thought-out and constitutionally viable alternative laws. New laws are now required to bring sensible limits to campaign financing but due to the divisions in Congress created by the two parties, it is very unlikely that they will be enacted. And the next cases of this nature on the Supreme Court docket will surely lessen or eliminate even more limits.

Have you noticed that many campaign restrictions are focused on the donor, not the candidate? The two parties do not wish to restrict themselves. A simple law restricting the income of candidates may be the answer here. Or how about a simple law that only allows donations from citizens in the district or state that the candidate is running in? Think Congress will pass one anytime soon as a response to these Supreme Court rulings?

In an unusual occurrence, Justice Thomas also wrote an opinion for the majority summarizing his beliefs that there should be no limits whatsoever in campaign donations and spending, declaring any such restrictions are unconstitutional.

In Justice Stephen Breyer's minority opinion he stated "If the court in *Citizens United* opened a door, today's decision may well open the floodgate." He also stated:

> Taken together with *Citizens United v. Federal Election Comm'n,* 558 U.S. 310 (2010), today's decision eviscerates our Nation's campaign finance laws, leaving a remnant incapable of dealing with the grave problems of democratic legitimacy that those laws were intended to resolve.[21]

Justice Breyer points out that before this decision, a rich donor could only contribute a maximum of $74,600 to political parties in a two-year cycle. Today, that figure has jumped to $1.2 million. Then he explains how a single donor can contribute $3.6 million to a single candidate from a maximum of $5,200 ($2,600/ea. for the primary and general election). Removing limits also allows for the creation of an infinite number of Political Action Committees (PACs) that can be used to funnel millions in donations from a single donor to a single candidate. This will be a common practice in "close" or embattled races.

There is no discussion how this ruling affects state or local office elections, but I can imagine that it would be advantageous for the special interests to invest large sums to these campaigns as well. It would essentially create a large basket of candidates from which to select the best one that fits their needs for higher office. History has shown that sometimes the outspent candidate wins the election, but the money does not need to win all the races, just a simple majority of each legislative chamber.

With all this money around to be given to candidates, it is obvious that most candidates must focus on obtaining some substantial funding to stay up with their future opponent. They are spending significant time on gaining and retaining their positions and not on solving problems or providing good governance. The Jury Party simply removes this from the equation. The financial requirements required by the two established parties in order to remain viable are simply not needed by the Jury Party. The jury Party needs people, not money. The Supreme Court made these decisions without regard to the grossly inferior position it places the American people in. The aristocracy of America is tightening the noose on the American people and the people are starting to choke. The Supreme Court will not even protect us. Only we can protect ourselves.

While the good guys far outnumber the bad guys, the biggest weakness of the good guys is the bad guys' cohesion—an individual is usually defenseless against the bad guys when they gang up. But if the good guys can come together and be united as a solid force for doing the right thing, the bad guys will back down. The bad guys have no real choice here—they know they are wrong and outnumbered; they cannot stand up to the decisions of a united and determined jury of their peers.

The Ninth Problem: Special-Interest-Run Government Results in Taxation without Representation

The ninth problem is that of special interests, which have clearly taken control of our government in many areas.

In many cases, the candidate for an elected position has a lot in common with certain groups of special interests. They form philosophical bonds, help define issues and legislation, provide campaign support and even form friendships. But after winning the election, the interest groups begin pushing for even more. The elected representative faces the fact that if he/she does not cooperate with these interests then he/she faces loss of support and defeat in the next election. The special interests have them right where they want them. The people have been removed from the system and we therefore literally have a system of taxation without representation.

Recently it was exposed that a non-profit organization called the American Legislative Exchange Council (ALEC) has great and undue influence over our state legislatures. Briefly, ALEC is a state-based organization of legislators and private individuals, 98% funded by non-legislator dues, that holds meetings between dues members and state legislators (approximately 2,000 legislators) to write and vote for bills that often benefit the dues-paying members. These bills are then promoted as state legislation and passed virtually word-for-word and state-to-state, which has given rise to the reference to ALEC as a "corporate bill mill." In return for the legislators' participation, they get an annual all-expense-paid vacation (to the national meeting) and get to talk to and gather significant financial campaign support from special interests outside their district. According to ALECEXPOSED.ORG, industries that benefit from this legislation include:

- Tobacco companies—bills limit lawsuits against them from victims of tobacco-caused illnesses.
- Pharmaceutical companies—tort "reform" prevents people from suing pharmaceutical companies that sell drugs with dangerous side effects.
- Private prison companies—this industry benefits from tougher drug laws and longer incarceration rates.
- Private Schools and Education companies—these institutions profit from laws promoting the privatization of schools.

The task force groups in ALEC include: Civil Justice; Commerce, Insurance and Economic Development; Communications and Technology; Education; Energy, Environment and Agriculture; Health and human Services; International Relations; Public Safety and Elections; and Tax and Fiscal Policy. In other words, this is essentially a shadow legislative assembly that works behind closed doors to advance their agenda. Unless you are a high-priced dues-paying member, you will not be a part of the legislative process.

So, what is ALEC up to lately? According to Suzanne Goldenberg, in her December 4, 2013 article in *The Guardian,* titled "ALEC calls for Penalties on 'Freeriders' Homeowners in assaults on Clean Energy,"[22] ALEC is engaging in a new offensive against homeowners who install solar panels. They are promoting legislation to penalize homeowners with solar energy panels and weaken state clean energy legislation. They are pushing legislation to reduce the mandatory compensation utilities must pay homeowners who generate electricity for the grid. In November of 2013, Arizona became the first state to charge a monthly bill to homeowners that have installed solar panels. Also in 2013, ALEC promoted 77 energy bills in 34 states that included efforts to reduce oversight of fracking operations, pushed for approval of the Keystone XL pipeline project, and opposed renewable energy. Many of the efforts were blocked in 2013 by overwhelming opposition by the citizens of these states, but now, according to the article, ALEC is focusing on a new strategy to weaken environmental and alternative energy laws.

You and I may even agree with some or most of their agenda—but that is not the point. The point is that ALEC is a very well-funded and organized special interest lobby that wants to influence your representative *without* your input. They may have lost last year, but they are simply regrouping, repackaging and starting a new offensive this year to move their agenda forward. Their strategy is to out-spend and out-last the opposition until they get their way by going behind the backs of the American people to gain influence with the people's representatives. Want to learn more? Go to ALECEXPOSED.ORG.

The rank-and-file followers of the opposition to this onslaught will be worn down eventually because they have a life to live, jobs to work, kids to raise, etc. We need a new system that will never allow these special interests to gain control of our representatives—*by design.* The Jury Party is attempting to create a system that never gets worn down, never capitulates and never releases control of their representative—and does this with little effort.

The Jury Party's actions to reduce or eliminate the influence of organizations like ALEC are simple and relatively easy. Each Jury Party group in a state house district investigates the special interest connections that their representative has. Now, you list those connections and the related legislation that he voted for, including the possible consequences imposed on the citizens, on an inexpensive flyer for distribution into every mailbox in the district during an upcoming election cycle. You also support a candidate that promises not to associate with such organizations. Imagine the look on your representative's face when he reaches into his mailbox and finds the flyer that exposes his connection to this corruption—priceless. And, for the most part, you're done. You have not only blocked ALEC and similar organizations, but you have possibly done so permanently. No more effort may be required, and it might be accomplished with as little as 1% of the voting age population in the representative's district, which will be explained later.

The Tenth Problem: The Current System Does Not Encourage Problem Prevention

The tenth problem is that there is no political profit in crisis prevention. Seriously, why would politicians in today's political system want to work hard to prevent problems? There is no glory in preventing war. If you want to prevent problems, wars and other crises, you must create a political system that rewards problem prevention. Some people might think that our leaders create crisis through incompetence or worse, just so they can project themselves to be the hero that solves the crisis. This idea may be correct to a greater or lesser extent.

What is the measure of a vibrant and effective society? I believe that measure, or judgment, comes from what society does to help its unskilled labor to succeed. If society fails to allow this group to be successful, then society suffers the consequences of high crime, degrading neighborhoods, personal depression, high medical costs and high incarceration rates. The jury concept, being inherently committed to the community and being representative of all the people, is better equipped to find value in local unskilled labor than national elitists' policies that favor the use of cheap overseas labor. With the Jury Party, the unskilled laborer has an equal say in how things are run and a voice to express his or her concerns. Our current elitist rule isolates this group from the decision-making process simply because it never interacts with all the people in the community and the unskilled workforce is not really adding much profit to their cause in the form of tax revenue and campaign donations.

Unskilled laborers have a voice as valid as, and equal to, that of any doctor, Wall Street banker, lawyer or engineer. They can clearly state what their problem is because they know it firsthand. The state does not have to hire a bunch of elitists to do a study.

Creating a society where people low on the economic ladder can recover from past mistakes or support families with limited skills will pay for itself many times over by preventing future crises. These solutions are not easy ones to accomplish and a great deal of trial and error must be used. Many communities throughout the country can make attempts and it will be important to keep excellent communications between communities to find what works best.

The Eleventh Problem: The Current System Fosters Division and Lack of Communication between Different Groups

The eleventh problem is isolation. Many groups—in particular ideological or economic groups, but also many others—seem to isolate themselves from all others. Industrialists do not talk to environmentalists; conventional doctors do not talk to alternative medical practitioners; liberals do not talk to conservatives; atheists do not talk to evangelicals and gays do not talk to straights. Another phrase for this is division between people or groups of differing viewpoints.

One of the starkest differences between the suburbs and small towns is the reduction in isolation in small towns. Suburbs, by nature, are isolated by class, generally divided by housing prices. Small towns, however, are more mixed. When you drive through the countryside, you may see a nice, obviously expensive home right next door to a rusty trailer. Rich kids often go to the same school as the poor kids, and so forth.

Isolation and division create ignorant bias due to the fact that the isolated person never hears, sees or experiences the alternative lifestyles, viewpoints and members of other groups. By 'experiencing the alternatives,' I mean the alternative viewpoints in politics, religion, class, lifestyle, health practice, etc.

I am not advocating that we all get mixed up—no. I am OK with everybody hanging with people whose interests they have in common, including wealth and social status. The issue is that when society tries to solve a problem or even tell people about the problem, the groups all tend to form a circle of wagons to support or attack the proposed solution. Generally, the different groups have no place or means to gather together and share the concerns and proposals for solutions to our problems. However, a system that forces people to share their experiences, fears and concerns and learn of others' experiences, fears and concerns is the way we can solve problems.

You cannot solve the crime problem, for example, unless the law-abiding citizens talk to reformed and enlightened former criminals to gain an understanding of why criminals do what they do. For example, criminals can tell you that they chose your house to rob because of the poor lighting, or they can say they started stealing because they were bored and unsupervised during high school and their experiences in the current juvenile justice system added to the problem. This can lead the community to make changes that can keep more students busy when not in school and implement improvements to the justice system.

This effort should not be given just to the experts, who are also isolated from all other groups, but ordinary citizens from all socioeconomic backgrounds existing in the community, listening to the criminals, the police, the psychologists and sociologists, having discussions among themselves and coming to a consensus of what to do to reduce crime without political agendas and fears driving the outcomes of such efforts. To do otherwise can be very costly and ineffective.

The Twelfth Problem: Authoritarian Enforcement Has Replaced Consensus of the Citizens

The twelfth problem is the way our current system and government leaders operate—the fundamental flaws in their methods of problem definition, solution development and execution of laws and regulations. We the people select or allow elites to climb to the top of the ladder with the promise of leading us to a better life. But this only works if we are lucky enough to have extraordinary people at the top. Elitists who climb to the top must make decisions and carry out enforcement of those decisions. In companies, managers can fire you, hold back raises or give you less desirable work to force compliance. But governments can tax you, fine you, imprison you, bankrupt you, or even execute you to get you to comply with the government's demands.

Such enforcement power does not necessarily attract pacifist type people, does it? Some, sure, but this power will also attract individuals or groups who need extreme power over people to satisfy their psychological flaws. If they cannot convince you they are right with words, then they will use law and police enforcement of their laws in a hopeless effort of creating a world in their image. The people usually recognize radical changes and rise up against such actions, but if done slowly and methodically, the people may not notice until it's too late to rebel peacefully.

However, what if all decisions were made by a jury of the people? A successful decision, even an unpopular one on a difficult problem obtained by a randomly selected, loyal and passionate jury and advancing their knowledge and understanding through several tiers, would be obtained through much discussion, research, scenario creation, conscious thought, predictive results, and mutual understanding of all sides. The jury would accept the decision because everyone on the juries involved would understand that it was the only or best decision to make. They would also know that they can tinker with the law as needed for improvements in the future. There would be little need for enforcement because the decision was made with the understanding and support of the people's true representatives, people just like them—not political party representatives far removed from the people and generally viewed as untrustworthy and disloyal to the populace.

It is also notable that a government decision, even if its solution to a problem is exactly the same as that of a jury, would be met with suspicion and opposition from the people who were not involved in forming the solution. Each side of the decision may make efforts to water down legislation, causing ineffectiveness and allowing the problem to continue to fester for years or decades. An authoritarian government would use force; put down street protest, jail activists or worse. This political battle occurs because the people do not have responsible charge of their community, state and country. Until now, no viable system existed for doing so.

The Thirteenth Problem: Politicians Are "Leaders," Not Representatives

The thirteenth problem I see is that we elect *leaders,* not *representatives.* There is a totally different mindset working here. Some legislators have openly come out and said the people elected him to be their *ruler*. They interpret the government established by our Constitution as an elected dictatorship; your freedom is dependent on which dictator you elect.

The mindset of leaders as rulers has its flaws. For one, the image of leadership must project the leader as never being wrong. When legislation is proposed, it is highly supported by the proponents and fiercely defended when passed into law. Leadership cannot fail and therefore the legislation is *always right* and must never be modified because it may lose its value by proposals from the opposition.

Is this the way you live and work? When you make a mistake in a decision that affects your home or work or that affects your budgets or schedule, do you stick with that decision because tinkering with it may result in bigger problems? Of course not! Human nature makes mistakes and human nature fixes things. When we realize a mistake as individuals, we fix it. When something falls apart we put it back together. When we miss our exit we turn around at the next one and get back on our path.

But when leaders in government make mistakes, they cover it up, put a spin on it, or ignore it. There is always an election coming up and they cannot allow their opponents to exploit their error. Our system allows mistakes to fester for decades and weaken our community and country until the next generation of leaders take charge and create a new round of festering mistakes.

When people become leaders, many of them rapidly fall into this trap. "Leaders" lose this aspect of humanity. They lose their ability to admit their mistakes and correct them for fear of looking like a failed leader.

One of the primary goals of the Jury Party described here is to fix mistakes honestly and quickly. Probably all legislation has poor aspects to it that require modification when exposed. Leaders will not admit these flaws but the people will. The people must live with government mistakes just as they live with their own personal mistakes and the Jury Party can provide the tools to fix the mistakes before they fester and damage our health and welfare. Jurors in the Jury Party are not leaders; they are just representatives executing the people's will. Millions of people discussing the flaws, discovering alternatives, promoting corrections and giving direction to their obedient representatives is the crux of the jury representative system described in this book. All you have to do is get involved.

The Fourteenth Problem: Government Leaders Habitually Hide the Truth from the People

All the above thirteen problems, along with many more that I'm sure you can offer, result in the fourteenth and largest problem with government today: *We do not know the truth.* I am absolutely positive and trustful that if the American people knew the truth of an issue, they could direct their representatives to make the right or best decisions—no question about it. But the problem is that we do not have a trustworthy source for the truth. History is clear: the government, corporations, media, you name it—they do not always tell the truth. They may tell their version of the truth, but they will leave off the opposing view that negates their argument. They fiddle with numbers; they avoid arguments, divert questions and bash their opponents—whatever it takes to promote the side they have chosen for their profit. Often, the debates on these issues are so confusing that the general population has absolutely no idea who to believe so they follow *image:* the image of confidence or some other character trait because the people have no idea who is right. This is typically seen in election debates where each side starts throwing numbers out to prove their side. If one candidate fumbles because he forgot his lines, he loses points that could lose the election resulting in a change in the course of history. Do you really want the future of our country and mankind to be dependent on this common scenario?

Is it even possible for our country, or any nation, to have good governance without a system that promotes the truth? Of course not! And our system often supports lies and deception, not truth. The Supreme Court even ruled in 2014 that political advertising or other methods of communication cannot be held liable for lying![23] Politicians can lie all day long and there are no consequences unless it becomes a media circus. In the Obama/Romney debates, both candidates were caught lying (typically through their version of the truth, never the whole truth) and it was no big deal because the American people were stuck with only two viable choices and the lies are heard and believed by more people than the revelation that it was a lie. And remember, these guys are very well versed in what to say in a debate.

Do you really expect success with such a system? Eventually, our nation will be doomed; there is no other possible outcome from a system that measures success by the leader's ability to get away with lying.

We are not the servants, they are; let's make that clear. These leaders who demand servitude from the people have been responsible for most of the wars, famine, economic failures, and even the dire consequences of certain natural disasters such as Hurricane Katrina, that have plagued the people for thousands of years. I want the aristocracy to step aside; it's time for the people to rule. The elite may have the degrees and experience, but the people have the common sense, knowledge and the experience of living under the rules first hand. The people have a better sense of the difference between right and wrong. It is the people who feel the hardships of the elite's decisions. The people should rule. All we need is a way to do it effectively with shared effort.

I don't believe that our problems really have anything to do with liberal vs. conservative, Republican vs. Democrat, young vs. old, poor vs. rich, educated vs. uneducated or white vs. black. Our problems are much deeper and more fundamental; they are the very foundations of the country. It is no longer philosophical issues that we must face, but system issues. The system is broken and we must now focus on the "system of government" and good governance. This effort includes all of us, with no exceptions, and we all need to get involved in fixing the system.

Chapter 5 — A Trusted System

> The two enemies of the people are criminals and government. So let us tie the second down with the chains of the Constitution so the second will not become the legalized version of the first. —*THOMAS JEFFERSON*

> Those who cast the votes decide nothing. Those who count the votes decide everything. —*JOSEPH STALIN*

> During times of universal deceit, telling the truth becomes a revolutionary act. —*GEORGE ORWELL*

What we want, what almost anybody wants, is a trusted system of government and institutions that provides valuable information and procedures for a community—a system of authority and a source of knowledge that is inherently trusted. A trusted system would have natural barriers that provide checks on corrupt and incompetent government officials and sources of information. Mistakes would be made, as they always are in a human-based system, but they would be quickly fixed without politically murdering those who made the mistake.

Is this possible under our current electoral representative process? No, it cannot happen because it would require constant and massive efforts and costs by the people without the advantages of a cohesive organization capable of mobilizing the people where needed.

During elections, we spend only *part* of our time paying attention to issues. We really do not have the time or attention span to delve deeply into more than one or two issues that determine who we vote for. Many times these few issues are conservative or liberal party agenda issues that influence our choice based on our personal party preference and have little or no impact on our lives. We often vote because we believe in our preferred party. Or our choice depends on how well an issue is sold with one-liners, irrelevant of whether it is right or effective.

How can we trust a system with this design? How do we go back to our busy hectic lives with confidence that our representatives are doing what is right to secure our future? Blind trust, that's how. For most of us, except perhaps community activists and cynics, we blindly trust the system. We have had the notion that, of all the lousy governments in the world, we have, even with all its flaws, the best government of all. This message has been crammed down our throats all our lives to justify its existence and actions or inactions, and advocate the support of the two-party system—a system, I repeat, that is NOT defined in the Constitution. It is time to focus, not on having the best government in the world according to our leaders and pundits (which is debatable), but a government that can be inherently trusted, period.

The way government officials look good is to make someone else, or another group, look bad. Lies and exaggeration are typical tools of an authoritarian political system, as well as fear, such as of a perceived enemy or threat, or an environmental or resource threat. If government can instill fear, it promotes trust in only itself and you have little choice but to follow. To spend the effort to find out that the trust is not real requires intense research and study—a very difficult effort to undertake amidst our hectic lives. Added to which, most government personnel would brush you off in such efforts, anyway. No, we need a system of government that is inherently trustworthy.

This book offers a system that puts the people in responsible charge. This system allows the people to make the decisions that impact their lives—decisions regarding tax and spend, cut and save, legalize or illegalize. It provides ample opportunity for people to speak out on issues, do detailed research, to make difficult decisions, voice complaints, learn the ropes and talk shop with their representatives in a constructive and effective manner. It forces the government to balance the budgets because in every group, someone will ask, "How will you pay for it?" and they will demand that this very important question be answered.

The current system makes most people ignorant because we only hear the slogans, biased reporting and slick ads. If the people get involved in government and the decision-making process, and learn what is really happening, that ignorance disappears quickly. Why? Because the responsibility is on *your* shoulders, not those of some politician that you can criticize for two, four or six years. The group of persons who are in responsible charge and are answerable to a knowledgeable, inquiring populace must justify every decision. They must be very well informed on the issues, the checks and balances, the costs and benefits, and the effects on future generations—not just the next election. When the justification of our foreign policy is "protecting American interests," we need a constituency that demands to know the specifics of what those "American interests" are. The mainstream media never seems to ask this question in the detail required by the people to formulate and express an informed opinion.

The people—who have a strong stake in their community, their city, their county, their state, their country and their world—are the best choice to make the difficult forward-thinking decisions required by governments today. It will be the people's children they hand their world over to in the near future and I trust they will do the right things and quickly fix a mistake when a poor decision is made.

Cohesion of the Community

What is the cohesion of a typical community? What brings a community together in a successful working unit? Why and how does a community enrich our lives? It's simple: communities bring people with different skills together for their mutual benefit. A few people out there want to be off the grid; they strive for independence from the perceived failings of the system, or just want to have the confidence of being independent. But there is only so much time to do this. There is too much to learn and know for this to be anything but a rare or temporary success.

Communities come together to share skills and resources. A successful community has many different people who each study a skill and become very good practicing that skill. An independent community contains doctors, engineers, teachers, police, firemen, builders, farmers, repairmen, road builders and people in many other professions which make it possible for the community to support the population. All these professions are dependent on being well trained and often rely heavily on outside sources of information, equipment or procedures.

Most individuals cannot perform well in multiple professions; they can't learn medicine, build houses, farm, and provide their own water and power without total dedication to the effort. Instead we rely on the people in other professions to do a much better job at skills we need than we could ever hope to do ourselves.

But how do we trust these professionals to be doing the best that can be done? How do we know that the doctor has been properly trained and updated on the latest techniques? How do we know that the builder is building according to the latest codes? How do we know that the latest codes are good enough for our community? How do we know that the teachers are using the best teaching methods or that their training is the best offered and they are getting good direction from administrators? How do we know that the history books our children learn from are accurate?

We have no choice but to trust the institutions that bring us all this knowledge and skill. We seek evidence of credibility such as diplomas, PhDs, top scholar awards, government studies, professional titles and the work of institutions or foundations that often have their own agendas. But who says they are right, honest or unbiased in their proposals? How do we know that all options have been considered or tried elsewhere? How do we know if the leaders dismissed valid alternatives to seek personal gain or to fulfill their biases?

We don't know. We have no choice but to trust the system currently in place. And if the system supports profit or bias over truth and integrity, then we are in trouble.

We need to be able to judge these institutions. We need to investigate, not just listen, to all sides and alternatives and be free to decide the best path forward. What better way to judge these institutions than by adopting the very institution that was developed for the sole purpose of finding the truth, the institution of the jury. Even with its human element of potential error, it is, by far, the most trusted institution in the history of the world.

The Jury Party works just like a successful community. It brings many people of various backgrounds together and creates cohesion within the group representing the community. It has the potential to create common goals and effective procedures for the community to progress in a trusted system.

I trust the people. I trust my neighbors and their neighbors. I trust my coworkers and their families. Sure, there are a few wackos out there on the fringe, but these fringe people need to be involved as well. Real change does not come from the mainstream; it comes from the fringe of society. From time to time, as the system in place becomes stale, corrupted, bloated or stagnates regardless of its past success, it is often the people on the fringe who see the problems first. People on the fringe see the errors of the system while the mainstream is focused on the successes and revels in the traditions and history that made their world great. Change, for the mainstream, is scary; they do not want to lose what they have built over the decades. But those on the fringe see the faults. Though sometimes misguided, biased or uninformed, they are still the first to see the errors of the system that will cause future failures.

There are many people in America who view the political parties as both corrupt and useless, but they have no alternative to resort to. After all, we have been programmed to believe that we have the best government system in the world, so we believe that it is best to leave well enough alone. Each party must keep fighting the opposition in a fruitless effort to maintain, change or change back, resulting in wasted efforts, costs and diminishing returns.

Is there a better way? Of course, there is always a better way of doing anything. New innovations are always improving the way we do things and this should apply to government as well.

The Truth of the Matter

The truth is an elusive thing. We listen to the authorities in the media and the government with skepticism, but we also believe them because there is no alternative, and to really believe them to be lying to us is to question the very heart and soul of America. Most Americans can't do that. They can constantly criticize these people and organizations, but when the rubber meets the road, they are nearly 100% behind them.

If we truly believe our government is lying to us on important issues that have the potential of costing us dearly in blood and treasure, then we question the purity and righteousness of our country. For many Americans this idea is unthinkable. Our patriotic loyalty is engrained in the American psyche, in our songs, in our holidays, our culture, our flag, the movies and our politics. Questioning America must be done very carefully so a person does not appear unpatriotic.

It is common and patriotic to believe that politicians are liars and the media is biased against America, but you can never say America is wrong. Well, if the politicians are liars and the media is biased, how can America be right? If the American people do not know the truth because of the politicians and media, then how in the world can the people be properly represented? How can the American people back government decisions when they do not believe they are getting the truth? The contradictions are obvious.

America and its people need a system that can find the truth, a system that holds the government to the fire, forces the truth to be told and does not rely on anyone but ourselves. Is such a system possible? Yes!

If by now you are thinking that the American people are not smart enough to rule their land, look at the following study. According to Richard Brake, co-chairman of the Intercollegiate Studies Institute's National Civic Literacy Board, in his article, "Opinion: Elected Officials Flunk Constitutional Quiz," 2011,[24] the Intercollegiate Studies Institute conducted a national survey of civics and U.S. Constitution knowledge to 30,000 Americans over a five year period, most of whom were college students, but which also contained a random sample from all education and demographic backgrounds. Included were 165 adults who had been elected to some office at least once in their lifetime, including local, state and federal positions.

The survey asked 33 basic civics questions and ten questions on the Constitution. Former elected officials scored 49% while ordinary citizens scored 54% on the Constitution part of the test. Based on this survey, random selection of a jury from the phone book would immediately improve the constitutional knowledge of elected officials by over 10%. Now, I think there are some really smart elected officials that probably scored very high on the test, from which we can only conclude that there was a very high percentage of former elected officials that scored very low. These low scorers constitute a significant percentage of your elected representatives. This survey evidences that your representatives are not the star performers you thought they were and that you have what it takes to rule your country; you just need the system that gives you a real voice and a reliable source of essential knowledge. The ten-question Constitution test is at the bottom of the referenced web page. Take it yourself and see how well you do.

Chapter 6 — Good Governance

The men who create power make an indispensable contribution to the nation's greatness, but the men who question power make a contribution just as indispensable .... For they determine whether we use power or power uses us. —*JOHN F. KENNEDY*

It may be necessary temporarily to accept a lesser evil, but one must never label a necessary evil as good. —*MARGARET MEAD*

Ordinary people, simply doing their jobs without any particular hostility on their part, can become agents in a terrible destructive process. —*STANLEY MILGRAM*

Let's take a look at what we really want from government. What should be the real goal of government? A critical look at the state today may imply that the state's goal is to grow and continue to take over many functions of society that used to be done by private organizations, local governments or individuals. If that is true, then when will it end? For this thinking is clearly unsustainable, in that eventually the government will take on too much responsibility to be efficient or effective, and the people will be taxed and regulated too much to be content.

What kind of government do people—do you—really want? Ignoring all the rhetoric in politics today and the liberal or conservative slant, what do you really want from government? Stop reading and think about this for a moment.

I think we all want good governance. Sure, you want it your way, everybody does, and if all policy is formulated your way, then that is icing on the cake. But if nothing goes your way, you still want the cake, right? The cake is good governance. Even if you are a Libertarian in a socialist system, if the system is very well run and you can speak your mind and act freely without retribution, you can have a good life.

What is good governance? Good governance is a government that effectively operates those systems and duties of the government that the people have given it the authority and direction to do. People want the government to run effective schools, reduce crime, protect the environment, maintain the peace, offer protection from those things and persons that individuals and communities cannot defend themselves from, provide fundamental economic tools, systems of commerce, etc.

These desires are not conservative or liberal; they are fundamentally shared by all people. So why are the campaigns so focused on conservative and liberal issues when they should be focused on the fundamentals? How do we get the politicians to focus on good governance?

The current system is based on good representation. If your representative did not vote according to the desires of the people, then you would vote them out of office. Simple enough—it should work. But it doesn't always succeed.

Politicians and political parties have learned to goose the system. They are elected by one-liners like "we are going to take care of your kids," "we are going to balance the budget," "we are going to defend our nation," "hope and change," or "we are going to cut taxes." They never say how they are going to do any of this or speak of the long term consequences of such actions. The devil is in the details and most candidates, parties, and movements rarely say how they will pay for any of their policies. They run on one-liners and hope they don't get caught with a tough question. The smart ones are able to deflect those tough questions by attacking their opponents. The election process has become a circus in which people vote on who appears to be the lesser of two evil clowns.

I don't want answers from politicians. In fact, I've come to expect little from the politicians because government is just way too big to be effectively managed by a bickering, career-driven group of a few hundred. What I do want is good governance. I want the politicians to be honest with the people, lay the cards on the table, get input from the people and then together with the people and government employees, develop answers that work without suffering the domination of special interest groups.

But many powerful politicians don't look for solutions, they just look for answers that appease the people, wheel-and-deal support for their pet projects and, typically, create profits for their financial supporters and their party. This process, of course, is unsustainable and unaffordable because there is no limit to the number of programs that are needed by the special interests. Our current system is a "system of the needy" in which every institution or group—rich and poor, liberal and conservative, Republican and Democrat—are needy.

My goal is simple: The people get what the people want and can afford; everyone has an equal say in all things governmental and an equal opportunity to say it.

Majority (Mainstream) vs. Minority (Fringe)

In order for there to be good governance, there needs to be a line of communication between the majority (mainstream or Democrats and Republicans) and the minority (the fringe, third parties or the disenfranchised). The mainstream usually runs things in society and the rank and file members generally do a good job. It is very difficult to convince them that they are wrong because they profit or expect future profits from the system they generally operate. Profits, in this case, include a paycheck, retirement, health insurance, etc. The mainstream leaders/politicians tend to isolate themselves from the forces of change by banding together and reinforcing their beliefs. They emphasize the overall success of society to defend the system from criticism, and simply ignore or downplay actual results (failures). The mainstream can focus attention on the changes for good that created the existing system, even though it was likely the fringe that was the force for the changes that the mainstream now takes credit for. If our founding fathers had been members of the mainstream, the Declaration of Independence and the Constitution may never have been written. In fact, many of our founders were part of the mainstream, but became disillusioned with the greed of an overbearing British parliament.

In today's America we have divided the mainstream into Democrats (liberal) and Republicans (conservative) as if they are the only people who exist. The network pundits usually fall into the extremes of these two groups, further confusing, dividing and isolating the American people. All the attention is focused on these two groups, yet there are many other groups out there—the groups I call the "canary-in-the-mine" groups. They are a small or perhaps not-so-small minority, warning about the errors of mainstream government and policy, devoted to their beliefs, possessing large and small followings to reinforce and confirm those beliefs.

The Occupy America and Tea Party groups are perfect examples. Only a few of these individuals are capable of defending themselves from the arguments of the mainstream and possess the skills to effectively express themselves to create doubt in the views of the majority. Many of their opinions are gut instincts and not based on good knowledge with the memory recall capability required to convince the majority. Their efforts usually result in severe criticism from the mainstream because they cannot adequately defend their positions. Some are even chosen by the mainstream media so they can be made an example of and humiliated on national TV. The supporters can repeat the movement's one-liners but they can rarely defend them thoroughly enough to merit credibility. Establishing the validity of their views and persuading and bringing others around to their point of view is a process that requires intense study and much time. Few people have the spare time and mental discipline to adequately address this. Thus, it is a major personal hurdle that constantly frustrates their passion.

This frustration can create a radical wing led by charismatic leaders or inner conniving groups that create a philosophy fueled by fear or other means. These radical wings are able to be created because these minorities are ignored by the mainstream. The minorities have little choice but to follow the radical wings and the "other" beliefs that the radical group develops. These radical groups, if well managed, are able to exploit every weakness and the errors committed by the mainstream parties and government. If economic or social upheaval occurs due to the errors or weaknesses of the mainstream, then the radical wing has the opening needed to take power and significantly change a country's future.

During these events, the mainstream population follows the radical wing simply because the leaders are very passionate about their philosophy and appear to know what they are talking about. During difficult times, the people follow passion, not common sense and reason. Later, all the improvements in the people's situation are credited to the radical wing, whether deserved or not. This radical wing often goes too far to the extreme by evicting the established aristocracy that knows how to get things done, often resulting in more upheaval.

How do we fix this? And we must fix it because the mainstream needs to hear the canary-in-the-mine minorities, or else our society will run itself off the cliff as other societies have throughout history. Listening to these independent minorities enables the society to avoid potential major interruptions in our progress like recessions, housing price collapses, corruption, resource interruptions and war. These independents moderate the existing system of laws and in so doing, can prevent these man-made disasters.

Who Constitutes the Mainstream?

In 1961, Stanley Milgram of Yale performed his now-infamous shock experiment in which selected people posing as teachers believed they were to, and were instructed to, apply increasingly painful electric shocks to a subject student each time the subject gave an incorrect answer to a question. The "teachers" believed they were giving shocks to the subjects, although the subjects were actors and no actual shocks were delivered. When the teachers administering the shocks hesitated or refused after hearing expressions of pain and distress in the subjects (who had been coached to make such expressions), they were urged and commanded to proceed with the shocks. The outcome of the experiment was that 65% of the teacher participants proceeded to deliver all shocks they were ordered to, up to and including the maximum 450-volt shock, even when it was against their moral misgivings and despite the protests, screams, apparent pain and distress of the subjects.[25]

I am proposing that these 65% make up the vast majority of the mainstream—they are the "me too" people, the people who do not want to rock the boat. Although fringe members may very well be a part of the 65% due to their naive, internal need for acceptance by authoritative figures, no doubt many of the participants in the experiment were members of the mainstream, or Democrats and Republicans, who play along with the system, follow the system leaders and buy whatever the leaders are selling.

The Jury Party will not please the mainstream initially. The Party will have to gain the attention and loyalty of the 35%—the one-third of the American people who do not accept authority on face value. With that success, the mainstream will join in, if only because they will no longer be "wasting" their vote on a third party—a typical excuse heard by mainstreamists. But is anyone really wasting their vote on third party candidates? How are you NOT wasting your vote if you continue to vote Democrat or Republican yet still believe that Washington does not represent the people?

I have coined this new word, "mainstreamist," which I have defined as *a person who is extremely loyal to the status quo; a person who blindly follows authority without seriously questioning its motives.* Also, this is *a person who works hard to understand and justify to others the motives and rules handed down by authority.* The mainstreamists are the "me-too" people—not stupid by any stretch and very knowledgeable and defensive of the status quo system currently in place. But they are very loyal, respectful and supportive of authority, even when authority goes terribly wrong. They are also the people who simply accept authority, knowing full well it is wrong. They are the ones who say "you can't fight City Hall." Well. In the Jury Party, you *are* City Hall.

Now, if 65% of the people are mainstreamist and follow orders, even with protest and uneasiness, and these same 65% are strong followers of the two mainstream parties, then who is Congress made of? Congress is made up of strong supporters and leaders of the mainstream, or the 65%. And what is Congress capable of doing or approving if told by "authoritative" figures (the president, top generals, party leaders, scientists, spy agency officials or other leading government figures) that a crisis is imminent if action is not taken? By logic, most members of Congress are mainstreamist also, which means our representatives will follow the country's leaders without very much questioning.

People who follow third parties or no parties are not members of the 99%, but are members of the 35%. Many of these 35% may exist in the eligible non-voting populace. The 35% need a system by which they can express themselves to influence the direction of society away from authoritative rule, to question authority, offer alternatives and be adequately educated to influence the mainstream. Who would you rather be ruled by? A person who follows authority or someone who always questions authority? If the people who question authority are our rulers, then they should always be questioning themselves and seriously consider the questions of the people.

Minds of Millions (M.O.M.)

What we need in this country is MOM. We need the *minds of millions* of people working on solutions to problems, not just following questionable leaders. And to implement this effort we need a system in place where all these people can work on the solutions that effect positive change.

Most decisions that are made today are proposed and campaigned for by leaders. These leaders exist in bureaucracies, scientific research groups, political parties, corporations, single-issue organizations and think tanks. They are led by very well-educated and informed persons who have some sort of an agenda based on their beliefs. We follow them because we have no other authority, because we trust our system to produce the very best decision-makers.

But do these leaders "think outside the box"? They view the world through blinders. Military advocates think the answer is force, diplomats think the answer is diplomacy, science advocates think the answers lie in their field and economists think the answer is economic policy. Then we ask our representatives, most of whom are often anything but experts in these fields, to decide which way to go.

I am proposing that the people, with a wide variety of experience and knowledge, will be better at filtering the information, analyzing the options and promoting a decision, sometimes a decision that "thinks outside the box." A system that promotes MOM will come up with better solutions. This theory will be proven with the Jury Party in the election of our representatives. Most representatives have brilliant, well-educated campaign advisers with proven track records that get them elected by diverting attention away from their faults or extreme opinions and promote a positive image for their candidates or their party's philosophy. The Jury Party eliminates image, campaign finance conflicts and party philosophy from the campaign and instead focuses on solutions to problems, issues and true representation. If the Jury Party can beat them in an election, then the theory is partially proven—the theory that the efforts of hundreds or thousands can outperform the efforts of superior individuals with large campaign budgets.

In the academic world this is commonly called "Cooperative Group Problem Solving." It has a proven track record of success and appears to be very helpful at solving problems and promotes the success of the group without compromising individual accomplishments. This method is currently promoted as an academic learning tool, not as a political system. The Jury Party could attract many experienced and knowledgeable advocates of this system in academics to assist in formal and practical applications in governing and common Jury Party practices. In this system, there are no charismatic individuals with "credentials" who have sole possession of the "soap box." Instead, everyone gets equal time to express their ideas in group discussions. And note that these are discussions or conversations, not just a comments period open to citizens that is mostly ignored by representatives. These "comment periods" (commonly seen at city and county commission meetings) are falsely viewed as democratic practices by the mainstream.

For a national issue, there may be several million people involved in the solution to a problem. Starting at the local level, in zip code or even sub-zip code areas, proposals for solutions will move up the levels, eventually getting into a national jury that will only put the final touches on the scope of the solution and resolve any conflicts between regions of the country. All issues pertaining to national security, economic matters, constitutional questions, or how the solution impacts the people, would be resolved because everyone will get a voice to express their ideas, fears or support. Only viable options with verifiable evidence will advance to the higher levels.

With MOM, we can prove that the people can govern their community, state and country effectively by developing solutions that meet the needs of the people and our nation.

Chapter 7 outlines a participatory system that works to bring people together to investigate problems, form policy and make decisions. This system produces a representative who is held to the will of the people.

Chapter 7 — Creating the Jury Party

Never doubt that a small group of thoughtful, committed citizens can change the world; indeed, it's the only thing that ever has. —*MARGARET MEAD*

As recent history has repeatedly shown, the right to vote, by itself, is no guarantee of liberty. Therefore, if you wish to avoid dictatorship by referendum, break up modern society's merely functional collectives into self-governing, voluntarily cooperating groups, capable of functioning outside the bureaucratic systems of Big Business and Big Government. —*ALDOUS HUXLEY*

The secret of change is to focus all of your energy, not on fighting the old, but on building the new. —*SOCRATES*

In the Introduction, I referenced two academic resources that I used to come up with the system of representation that is the foundation of the Jury Party, *Random Selection in Politics* by Lyn Carson and Brian Martin, and *Is Democracy Possible?* by John Burnheim. In addition to these two books, this chapter will discuss the work of the Jefferson Center of Minneapolis, MN, an organization that actively promotes and manages randomly selected juries that judge public policy.

Carson/Martin make this argument in their book:

> The assumption behind random selection in politics is that just about anyone who wishes to be involved in decisionmaking is capable of making a useful contribution, and that the fairest way to ensure everyone has such an opportunity is to give them an equal chance to be involved.[26]

Equal chance also means that they have done research or have personal experience with the subject at hand, or else their opinion may be of little value. The Jury Party should include Project Juries that focus on specific issues or pending legislation. Project jurors are randomly selected members from a group of people who have stepped forward with an interest in the issue. Project juries can be the primary groups in a jury group with the Jury Party organization simply coordinating the efforts of the Project Juries.

The Jefferson Center's method of random selection involves intense polling and demographic selection, due to their method of selecting one jury.[27] It would be time-consuming and costly to select the number of jury members required to adequately police all aspects of government by this method. The jury selection proposed in this book begins locally in a much smaller and less diverse group. As described below, the process of climbing up the ladder to congressional or state levels requires the acceptance of their fellow jurors and group volunteers; essentially they are interviewed and supported based on their performance in lower, local tiers, as well as through the luck of the draw.

The jury system described by the Jefferson Center handbook can involve as much as 1900 effort hours of administrative support to complete a jury effort for one issue. That is clearly unaffordable, and thus will require that individuals in the Jury Party proposed here need to become knowledgeable about the workings of a simplified jury system. Through this system the costly selection methods utilized by the Jefferson Center can be avoided.

The Tier System

Following are suggested step-by-step instructions for getting this system underway: developing the Jury Party organization, selecting a representative, implementing state constitutional amendments and forming the Project Jury. Note that these steps describe the people's participation in tiers or levels.

The 1st tier local jury groups are strictly randomly selected. Through a combination of voting and random selection methods suggested below, the 1st tier members select representatives to the 2nd tier, and the 2nd tier members select representatives to the 3rd tier and so forth. Also, for the election example, I am focusing on the U.S. House of Representatives because most of us can relate to national issues and the tier system is better described using this national body of representation. But the tier system can be used for any elected office, and even cabinet positions, amendments to state constitutions and judicial appointments.

Tier systems will need to be developed for the state party and for each public office, customized for your area or state's demographics. I would suggest that the first efforts, after the state party or a large region of your state is formed, be focused on electing city councilmen, county commissioners, sheriffs, and state legislators. We need to emphasize local success and then move up the ladder. As people recognize the quality of our local elected officials, they will be more accepting of state and then federal office candidates. Knowledge in local and state issues will better define what is needed on the federal level. And local officials have better communications with state and federal officials to present issues and opinions of the people. Local officials also have influence on getting qualified people, such as college professors, state bureaucrats or business professionals, to provide testimony on issues that are important to their constituents to create a more informed debate. Local officials should be able to obtain information from bureaucracies, corporations, colleges or banks because of their positions or titles, and they can state that the information is for "a study" they are doing for their area. These information sources play an important role in justifying your position on issues.

Here is a brief outline describing the tier system:

1st Tier—formed from members in one zip code. (There is a wide range of population in many zip codes and this will need modification for some areas. For some zip codes or representative districts, sub-tiers will be required or a combination of several zip codes will be needed to form one tier.)

2nd Tier—formed from six to twelve 1st Tier zip code groups. (This tier may be your city or county tier.)

3rd Tier—formed from six to twelve 2nd Tier groups. (This tier might encompass all the zip codes in a federal congressional district.)

Let's Take it from the Top

To avoid possible confusion as you read the steps in the next sections, maybe we need to look at how this system could work from the perspective of a completed jury type system of representation on the Congressional level—that is, from the top down. In our example, a Congressman from the Jury Party has been elected. (In this example we will make some numeric assumptions to simplify the math; the numbers of jurors mentioned aren't necessarily the same as there would be in actuality.)

Let's take a situation where an industry requires some favorable legislation. This may take the form of a single line in a 100-page bill allowing a loophole that will reap tens of millions in profits annually for the industry. The industry hires a lobbying firm, sometimes made up of former Congressmen themselves, that begins the process of luring about a half dozen members of Congress. These Congressmen are high ranking members of the committee and sub-Committee the legislation is concerned with, or they are leading members of both or just one of the political parties. The lobbyists will wine and dine these key members, promising campaign donations and/or providing all-expense-paid trips to a tropical paradise for a quick meeting.

The lobbyists will do whatever it takes to influence these members to alter or pass a piece of legislation that generates huge profits for their clients. If the high ranking members buy the idea, they start putting the pressure on the other members of Congress to get a majority. Remember, there is a reason these lobbyists are in Washington—because it is very profitable. How does the Jury Party change this scenario?

If these lobbyists approach your Jury Party Congressman with offers for trips to Bermuda the Congressman simply tells them that his jury of twelve dictates whether or not she will vote for the law. So the lobbyists approach the Congressman's jury to wine and dine them to their point of view. But after a series of five-course dinners, the Congressman's jury tells the lobbyists that their vote on the legislation is dictated by their 2nd tier jury members, who they represent. So the lobbyists wine and dine 144 jurors in the 2nd tier. But the 2nd tier jurors, after eating their pizza, tell the lobbyists that their vote is dictated by their 1st tier jurors. Now the lobbyists must wine and dine 1,728 jurors (boxes of donuts this time). Now, what if half the juror in the first tier have to report to a sub-1st tier jury, such as might be found in densely populated zip codes. In this case, the lobbyist must wine and dine an additional 10,368 jurors. With what? Coupons?

Now multiply that number by a hundred or more Congressmen and I think you can realize the problem the Jury Party will be for lobbyists and any other special interest groups that may want to influence Congress. And even after the lobbyists influence hundreds of thousands of jurors to get passage through the House, they must start all over again with a Senate that has a whole different group of jurors.

And realize this is only possible if all those jurors agree to the influence. If any juror exposes the corruption, the whole effort may collapse and the industry the lobbyists were serving will get a poor reputation that may take years of hard honest work to overcome.

Another scenario might be that the industry advertises or promises jobs to the large populated states with the most

Congressional members so as to influence the people that make up the juries that will decide the issue. Assuming that the jurors do not thoroughly investigate this bill, the industry might win. But then there is the obstacle of the Senate, where the lower populated states will see no profit from accepting the legislation.

I'm sure this system is not fool-proof; these special interest groups have very smart people working for them. But you must admit the challenge could be so daunting that the special interests will find other ways to expand their markets and profits—perhaps the way most people do, with good honest hard work and proper management of their money.

The 26 Steps Leading to the National Jury Party Organization

Below are the steps suggested to progress from a zip code level organization to a national organization. The steps listed below are for an average size state with about six Congressional House members. If you live in a larger state, such as California, you will need at least one more level. Or if you live in Wyoming, then you may need one less level. Each state needs to review how you will get from the zip code level to the state level.

Step 1. Sign up

- Go to the website JURYPARTY.ORG and sign up for membership. Initially, there will be a page where you can enter your zip code, state, city, county, email address and State and Congressional District number; later the state senate district, commissioner, city councilman precinct and so forth will be added. There is no cost or obligation, and no flood of emails will be sent to you—we do not sell anything, except this book of course, which supports the website.

Step 2. Membership reaches milestone in zip code

- When enough people sign up in your zip code—about 24 (or 100 in a slow growth congressional district)—the website will send you an email notice stating this, which means it is time to get together with your neighbors. This email indicates that people want to organize. You may be inclined to be one of the first or maybe wait and join later. A second email will be sent letting you know who your contact is for meeting information if, and when, you decide to participate. No pressure.

- Note: An alternative path is to form the congressional district first and then work your way down to the zip code groups as membership grows. If you only have enough members to start at the congressional level, about 100 members, then you may want to focus on organization aspects of your congressional district and work with other congressional districts to create the state level. As membership increases, divide the congressional district into about six sections to form the next lower tier. When the zip code memberships reach 24, the congressional level will be able to provide much needed guidance to get things going quickly. From the congressional level, you may also want to:

- Investigate your representatives' (congress, state house, city and county) voting records, speeches, block voter support, special interests ties and financial support. Analyze the vote records and special interest relationships of your representatives. Find a pattern, if one exists.

- Create a party introduction flyer describing the Jury Party with some of your findings to be distributed in mailboxes or cooperating businesses. Distribution of these flyers might give your district a significant boost to membership that would allow the zip code groups to form.

- Make absolutely certain that anything put into a flyer is the truth, the whole truth and nothing but the truth. Verify, verify and then re-verify. If the verification is questionable, then include a statement saying that further research is needed.

- Form the structure of the tier system in your district. You can begin by breaking up the district into six lower tier groups of zip codes. Then progress from there as membership increases.

Step 3. Someone instigates a meeting

- Someone, maybe you, will set up a meeting place for your zip code; it's first come-first serve here. This person is not automatically the leader, just someone who takes the first step. The location can be a school, church, bar, restaurant, hotel meeting room or someone's house —it doesn't matter where. The email is sent to everyone in the same zip code. The person who begins the process may include a pressing issue or a list of issues that he/she feels compelled to address, instead of organizing to change your representative as described here. Another good reason to meet is to get the state party organization started.

Step 4. Time to Meet

- The first meeting will be a bit chaotic, but in every group there is always someone who tends to lead. Perhaps you will meet in a number of small groups to get a handle on your mission and share some information about yourselves. Get a count of people to see if there can be more than one 1st tier group. I'd say there should be no more than fifty active members per group initially. Later, as the group is better organized, larger memberships will be possible.

- Eventually there will be online brochures that help with organizing these events. Keep in mind that you are welcome to be a wallflower. There should be no pressure to do anything; it's on a strictly volunteer basis. If you want to just sit and watch, go ahead.

Step 5. Discuss issues and goals

- Talk about issues, talk about your lousy political representative(s), talk about whatever comes to mind and set the goals of the group.

- Goals can include research on specific issues, organization to the state level, digging up information on your current representatives or making sure the Jury Party has a voter guide for people to use when voting.

Step 6. Select facilitators

- Select two facilitators, because you do not want to overwork one facilitator and two facilitators can back each other up if things get out of hand. The facilitators are important and should have a good background as a manager, arbitrator, teacher, etc. Government experience is a plus. They also must stay out of the fray and be very neutral in their opinions. Facilitators keep things going and make sure no one gets bored or alienated, so choose wisely. Unlike media moderators, they are not there to provoke controversy and dissension.

Step 7. How does this group function?

- Set up the methods for getting the group working. The facilitators will lead this effort. You must do at least the following:

- Discuss how a group of 6-12 jurors will be selected from members willing to serve. This is the group that makes the decisions. I strongly suggest using random selection exclusively, like a jury, because you do not know your fellow members well enough to make good selections at this point.
- Discuss the rules and write them down, including when to open discussions, the agenda,

etc. Create a list of bylaws from these rules that your tier and your tier's representative(s) will abide by. You may have a bylaw that says your representative(s) will never vote for or against an issue or legislative bill without consulting the tier they represent. Be sure the bylaws put the members of the tier in control of their representative(s).

- Schedule meetings and locations; spread them around the zip code area. I suggest weekly at first, then more or less often as necessary. Investigate the effectiveness of some meetings being done through the internet, saving valuable travel time for members.

Step 8. Select jurors

- Select your six-to-twelve jurors for this group from the people in the group who wish to be jurors. Again, random selection allows all people a chance to be empowered. We do not want to allow image to influence our choice at this stage. Just drop the names into a box of those who are willing to serve and draw six to twelve names. It might also be a good time to randomly select a head juror from the jury, not to rule or even lead the proceedings, but to be the go to person that other jury leaders or outsiders could contact and coordinate business with. This position may also be better held by one or both of the facilitators. Or even someone who is not a facilitator or juror, but just a member, thereby ensuring that this position will not overwork someone who has already been assigned responsibilities.

- Note: this is your base level jury group. That is, all other jury paths begin here. For example, this group combines with other groups to form the city councilman jury consisting of all the zip codes in the councilman's district. The zip code jury is the starting point for progressing to the state representative jury, the state Jury Party as discussed here, the U.S. Congressman jury, county commissioner jury and most others.

Step 9. Work issues

- Set up projects for the group to work on. I suggest that at least one member of the jury, and people from the audience in a number manageable for the effort required, be included in each project group. A great deal of information must be obtained and verified, so try to select the right number of project members to get the work done in a timely manner. These projects may include: setting up a website for your group, digging into your representative's campaign finances, getting your representative's voting records and speeches, discussing current events and what your expectations are, reviewing a legislative bill proposed in Congress or your state house, etc.

Step 10. Connect with neighboring zip code groups

- Select members of your group to talk to other zip codes' 1st tier groups to keep each other informed about the main issues the groups are discussing and how well you are organizing your group. Be sure to share your bylaws with other groups to create some uniformity between adjacent zip codes. Compare each group's discoveries that are made in your investigations. This will help a great deal if your group is not progressing as well as others. You will want to progress at about the same speed as other neighboring zip code groups. You must also begin to think about how zip code groups will be joined to create the 2nd tier.

Step 11. Group the 2nd tier

- When considering how to group zip codes into 2nd tier groups, it will be important to not create groups that have economic, racial, ethnic, political or lifestyle uniformity. Doing so might create barriers to a unified district that can and probably will cause major delays progressing on issues or policies. The following should be thought through:
    - Consider travel distances required to attend meetings by members.
    - Consider economic differences with the intension of getting a good cross section of economic levels in your area.
    - Consider ethnic and racial differences with the intension of getting a good cross section of ethnic, racial or religious groups in your area.

- Consider political party voting histories. Do not divide up into groups of zip codes that have a strong loyal Republican or Democrat vote history.
- Consider having some rural, suburban and urban areas in each group, if possible.

Step 12. Select 2nd tier jurors

- Select two representatives from your 1st tier jury and representatives from all other 1st tier groups in the 2nd tier area to become 2nd tier jurors. The 2nd tier will again consist of about twelve jurors from about six 1st tier groups. Your selection of the 2nd tier members should be a combination of votes and random selection.

  For example, you could hold a vote and then randomly select two from the top four vote-getters. Or, allow the jurors to vote for all the qualified jurors. That is, if you are a juror and you think five of your fellow jurors are qualified to be promoted, then place all five names in the pot to be drawn. This way, the jurors who have gained the most respect from their fellow jurors have a better chance of winning the draw. The person who wins (or loses) has no idea whether they got one vote or eleven votes. There is no debt to repay or desire for vindication. The winner knows they have to step up to the position and please all jurors because they do not know what their level of support was. Also, randomly select their replacements on the 1st tier jury.

- In rural communities, your 2nd tier and 3rd tier representative will probably need gas money and even hotel and food allowances. Have members donate accordingly and have two randomly selected treasurers keep track of donations and expense reports. Urban areas may not need any expenses, but still need the cost of equipment or a large meeting room rental. Every group will need a printer and supplies to print out informative flyers or handouts of the agenda at meetings. Even consider a booth at local festivals or political events to promote the Jury Party. Each location judges the needs of the group, but it is very important that there will be zero tolerance for fraud. *Do not* suggest dues to join this organization—that will discourage many people from joining, which would defeat the purpose of the organization.

Step 13. Consolidate 1st tier issues and bylaws

- While the 1st tier groups continue with what they were doing before, the 2nd tier groups consolidate the views, desires and opinions of the 1st tier groups. And, importantly, they consolidate the bylaws of the 1st tier groups into the bylaws of the 2nd tier, which should be approved by all the 1st tier groups represented. The 2nd tier focuses on the issues that were or are being worked on in the 1st tiers. The 2nd tier may decide to go into further investigation, and even call in witnesses or expert testimony, on the issues most important to them. They may form project groups that go even further into detail, just like what was done in the 1st tier groups. This group should retain two of the experienced 1st tier facilitators to oversee the meetings and functions of the 2nd tier.

- One warning I'll make here is to avoid traditional liberal and conservative lightning-rod issues like abortion, gay rights, gun control, welfare, immigration, etc. These issues will only divide people and misdirect the focus away from good governance. These issues can be taken up later after this system is well established and our experiences improve our procedures, interaction skills and judgments.

- Eventually, should this system succeed, the lightning-rod issues will come to the forefront of discussions. These conservative/liberal issues will need to be resolved eventually—not by the politicians, but by the people. Each side must sit down with the other and argue their points. Hammer out a compromise, write legislation and give it to the state and federal legislatures for passage or judge the merit of a legislative bill or amendment to the state constitution. This kind of effort should quell the issue for a while until the next generation of young voters, brought up under the law, decide to change it. Cultural and moral values change as arguments are refined and clarified.

- These social issues need to be settled *by the people who must live with their decisions,* not by the government, because the government will resist changing a law without overwhelming demands from the people and years of discussion and delays. These social issues are cultural street fights, after all, and should not be determined by an all-powerful government full of egotistical, self-righteous, biased and bought-off politicians who are judging whether to take up the issue based on the benefits to the party and the next election.

- Experience in this system will give us the qualities and abilities necessary to effectively discuss these emotional issues. And, with success at thinking "out of the box," I'm certain that many of these issues may be resolved with answers that are not even viewed as liberal or conservative. Emotions will be tempered and successful solutions should prevail—but that is all in theory. I can't wait to find out what really works on these types of issues.

- If a lightning-rod issue is front and center on people's minds due to a proposed state constitutional amendment, for example, then do have discussions through a Project Jury—but with the mutual understanding that discussions will be somewhat arduous and tempers need to be controlled. The facilitator of these discussions will have to be very cognizant of potential flare-ups and all sides need to respect the facilitators when they direct the group away from a hot topic until the next meeting after people have cooled off. Remember not to lose touch with the group's fundamental purpose: for the people to gain the upper hand with government.

Step 14. Connect with other neighboring 2nd tier groups

- Same effort as step 10 above in the 1st tier group. Select members of your group to talk to other 2nd tier groups to keep each other informed with the main issues and how well you are organizing your group. Compare the bylaws and agenda of each group to ensure compatibility.

Step 15. Group the 3rd tier

- You may consider geography to minimize travel time and cost by your selected representatives or demographics like you did creating the 2nd tier above. But you also may consider the district of your state or federal representative as well. This jury level may be the group that has a direct line to that representative. Plan ahead how this will affect the state level.

Step 16. Select 3rd tier jurors

- Now form the 3rd tier by selecting two 2nd tier members from each group through votes and random selection. Random selection keeps the aggressive power seekers from dominating the selection. We want ordinary people doing extraordinary things here. Keep the number of jurors of the 3rd tier group at about 12-20. The more members you have, the more facilitators you should have.

Step 17. Consolidate 2nd tier issues and bylaws and incorporate 3rd tier rules

- Same effort as the 2nd tier group in Step 13. Consolidate the bylaws into a clear set of rules and incorporate 3rd tier level rules into them.

- Note that the consolidation effort will be performed by the new representatives of the 2nd tiers who will try to create a united group. These representatives should stay in constant contact with the 2nd tier they represent and get any 3rd tier bylaws approved by their respective 2nd tier jury.

Step 18. Connect with other 3rd tier groups in the state

- Same effort as steps 10 and 14 above. Select members of your group to talk to other 3rd tier groups to keep each other informed with the main issues the groups are discussing and how well you are organizing your group. Compare the bylaws and agenda of each group to ensure compatibility.

Step 19. Select state-wide jurors from the 3rd tier groups

- Now form the state party by selecting two 3rd tier members from each 3rd tier group through votes and random selection.

- I think that most meetings and discussions of the state group can be done on the internet. Some travel may be required like an annual convention of some sort. Also, travel to neighboring states may be required as you develop your regional groups.

Step 20. Consolidate 3rd tier issues and bylaws

- Same as before. You may not need facilitators at this level. The state level will have very experienced jurors that should be able to manage things themselves but will work closely with their 3rd tier jurors and can get help from their 3rd tier juries as needed.

Step 21. Connect with other state parties in your region

- Connecting with neighboring states begins the process of consolidating issues and bylaws. Each state will be different and some compromising efforts will be required.

- Also, not all states will be creating their state levels at the same time so you may want to connect with some 2nd or 3rd tier levels in other states to let them know how and what you are doing—keep in touch.

Step 22. Select state jurors for regional jury

- When all your neighboring states have their state parties it will be time to create regionals. Logically, the regionals will include the southeast, northeast, mid-Atlantic, midwest, northwest and southwest. This grouping will create a 12 person jury for the national party.

Step 23. Consolidate state level issues and bylaws

- We will have to use conference calls and internet meeting programs to reduce travel cost. Remember that there is no formal funding for these things within the Jury Party.

Step 24. Connect with other national regions

- Just as with lower tier groups—stay in touch and keep a pulse on what is going on.

Step 25. Select jurors for national party jury

- Use a combination of random selection and voting

Step 26. Consolidate regional level issues and bylaws

- After this effort there will be a national agenda. The agenda may not necessarily be issue oriented at this time but may be organizational in nature. It will take time and study to set the agenda on issues. The Jury Party seeks the truth and a consensus from all opinions can be very time consuming.

- Each tier level decides issues and forwards these decisions to the next upper tier who take on the issue. If an argument needs verification by the state level jury, then the juror requesting the verification that requires investigation can make a request to a lower level tier. Possibly, the investigations could be always sent to the 1st tier jury to create a Project Jury for the study. These investigations can be performed by multiple 1st tier juries throughout the state and move up the tiers, confirming the findings, until it reaches back to the state level.

- This example selects two jurors to represent each tier because this creates the levels to the national party. After this, all jurors should be selected for two-year terms so that a new juror is selected every year. This will mean that half of a jury will be replaced with new jurors every year for a two-year term. This way, half the jury has the experience to keep things going without interruption.

And that is the basic setup for the national party. Obviously, the details will be developed as we grow and changes will be needed. A constant vigil will be required by people who are passionate about organizations during this process of development.

The 8 Steps of Project Juries

Project juries are the groups that answer questions, investigate the candidates for office, delve into issues of concern, review legislation and solve any organizational problems that may occur. Project juries are where the work gets done.

Step 1. A zip code group forms a Project Jury to study an issue

- Randomly select the project jurors that will lead the effort from the list of members that want to be included. At least one juror from the zip code jury should be included on the Project Jury.

Step 2. Research the problem or issue

- List possible solutions to study
- Do research, such as has this problem been solved elsewhere?

- List the solutions with the pros and cons for each solution. Be sure to back up each solution with factual evidence.
- List the resources so others can verify.

Step 3. Present your findings to the zip code jury

Step 4. Decide to move forward with one or more possible solutions if required

Step 5. Contact other zip code juries and present your findings and request participation, if the project involves those zip codes.

Step 6. Forward the proposal to the 2nd tier jury and to subsequent levels until you reach the tier level that the Project Jury was intended for (such as a county, city, group of counties, state, regional or national).

- The purpose of the 2nd and higher tiers is to consolidate the findings from the many parallel 1st tier efforts and determine the need for any further investigation if there are stark differences in the findings of the groups.
- The purpose of multiple 1st tier groups investigating the same issues is to verify that the findings of the groups are consistently accurate. If differences are

found, then the differences are discussed and more research needs to be done for the differences to get settled.

Step 7. Create an open system where such creative and civic minded people can propose Project Juries to any level of the tier system.

- These higher tier juries can then forward the proposal to the lower tier juries to gain participation where required.

- For example, if a private state organization wants a state-wide investigation on an issue, they might go to the state party to make the request. Then the state party might organize the effort, break down the effort into manageable parts, and send the request down the tier levels until it reaches the 1st tier for the actual investigations to begin.

Step 8. If a program becomes a reality, then the Project Jury becomes a permanent jury organization until the problem is fixed.

The Project Jury may even remain in existence and operate similar to a tier group to monitor the success and implement innovations and improvements. The Project Jury can become essentially a standards committee that oversees a program, constantly receiving feedback and making recommendations to the agencies or the legislature, such as: acceptable police procedures while serving arrest warrants or standards of privacy which may change depending on the latest uses of technology or scuffle with the paparazzi. These Project Juries can, when accepted as a permanent jury, change their designation to "standards juries" to reflect what their actual purpose is. Project juries can be the designation for juries that are created to solve a problem or answer a question, and they are then disbanded when their mission is accomplished.

The project and standards juries are the think tank and heart of the Jury Party. These juries are where the answers to our problems will come from. The Jury Party organization reviews the results of the project and standards juries and votes on whether to support the results or not.

State Constitutional Amendment Steps

Step 1.

An outside group proposes an amendment to the constitution and asks for Jury Party support, or the amendment is proposed by Jury Party members.

Step 2.

The proposed amendment may be forwarded to any level of the Jury Party. If supported by a favorable vote by the jurors according to the bylaws, then that level forwards the amendment to lateral, higher or lower levels for consolidation or further investigation through Project Juries.

- ***Example:*** Amendment is proposed to the state party jury. The state party jurors support its consideration for passage and then forward the proposal to the 1st tier juries for study to be sure the amendment is good. A list of investigations that require Project Juries is created by breaking down the amendment into manageable parts. The proposed amendment, if successful, moves up the tier level and eventually reaches the state level where, if approved by the state jurors according their bylaws, it becomes a part of the state Jury Party platform.

- ***Example:*** Supporters of a proposed amendment petition a number of 1st tier juries to review and support their cause. If approved by the 1st tier jurors and there is with enough interest to study the proposal by their members, the 1st tier groups study in detail the amendment in Project Juries and move the amendment to the 2nd tier where arguments for and against are consolidated and studied further, if required. When the decisions of these levels reach the state level, then the amendment is voted on by the state jurors based on their constituent's recommendations to determine whether the amendment will be supported by the state platform.

- If a Jury does not support the amendment, but other lateral juries do, then this jury must make arguments against the amendment. Depending on the final judgments of the state level jury, the amendment passes or fails according to the bylaws that govern passage of amendments. Bylaws are very important in this jury process to ensure no biased results.

Step 3.

With widespread support for the amendment, the state jury passes approval and supports the amendment. Each zip code jury group adds this amendment to their list of amendments to support and spreads the word.

- Amendments to state constitutions may be a great example of the power of the Jury Party. A vast number of people would be available to sign the petition to get the amendment on the ballot if the Jury Party supports it. For many sincere movements promoting amendments, the Jury Party may be the easiest and least costly effort to get the amendment on the ballot. But amendments supported by special interests for their profit may have to go the arduous and expensive usual method with the realization that, without the Jury Party support, the amendment will have difficulty passing.

17 Steps to a Congressional Election

The steps below describe a possible method for selecting a candidate for a U.S. House seat, but these same steps can be used for any elected office.

Step 1.

At some point you must conclude whether your representative(s) are good or bad. If they are good guys, then the group may send letters to your representative about key legislation before Congress.

And, by all means, let your congressman know what he/she is doing right. They may come to one of your meetings and stay in better communication with your group than other groups they typically meet with due to your interest and knowledge of the issues. They may also be under pressure to toe the party line and bend to special interest groups on issues that your group has strong opinions about. You will provide a large, active group that can support your representative and give them the courage and knowledge to stand up to these special interests.

In the above case, since your congressman is an OK person, move on to local candidates, state representatives or state and U.S. senators. I think we should delay discussing the national executive branch at this time to avoid looking like a typical third-party organization. Go to step 2 and substitute another elected official for the word "congressman" and use Project Juries to organize the tier levels accordingly. Your tier level base is the zip code groups, and tier group paths need to be created by you for each elected office according to your demographics.

Step 2.

If your group determines that your congressman is a bum and has got to go, coordinate your feelings with other local 1st tier (zip code) groups in your district.

One important note: Your zip code may think your rep is a bum but another zip code may think he is great because the rep caters to that zip code's voter block. This is a huge obstacle early in organizing that needs to be overcome quickly. Negotiate, form joint juries, do whatever it takes to bring the zips together as one voice. Perhaps the representative will change his or her mind on a few issues that will alter your attitude toward him/her. Perhaps you can convince the other zip code group that he or she is, in fact, a bum. Do this with the attitude that someone, maybe you, is missing something about this representative that needs to be addressed.

Step 3.

Break up into groups to assess your congressman's opponents in the upcoming election; hopefully you will be in time to affect the outcome of the primary elections. Present what your subgroup has found and discuss the pros and cons of each candidate thoroughly amongst the whole group. Do not allow conservative or liberal bias to derail a potentially viable representative—more on why this is important later.

Step 4.

Select one or more of the congressman's opponents who meet your criteria for a good representative. Get the opponent to come to your meeting, or a joint meeting with several zip groups. Explain who you are and what you want as a group. Make them convince you that they deserve your support.

Step 5A.

You are convinced that this opponent can be supported by your group. Go to step 6.

Step 5B.

They are all bums. We must select candidates from our group and run a Jury Party candidate. The process is the same except that there will be no primary election. Go to step 9.

Step 6.

Review your bylaws and make sure that they include how the candidate for Congress that the Jury Party is supporting will interact with the Jury Party. You may include bylaws that require the congressman to hold a two-hour weekly meeting with the jury members to discuss upcoming legislation, that develop Project Juries that require legislation investigation or which discuss the people's feelings about current events.

During these regularly scheduled conference or internet calls, your congressman can also use this time to inform you of how Washington really operates—good stuff that will give you inside information when talking to your peers. You will be the person people listen to because you know the scoop of what is going on in Washington from the Congressman's perspective, not the garbage that most people hear on the cable shows. They will ask you how you know all this stuff and that is your opening to sell the Jury Party. Many will check out the website and some may join. The larger your group, the more voters and campaign supporters you have. More people also bring in more experience and insight as to how the government should be run and enable more investigative Project Jury groups to be formed.

Another important bylaw is to let the congressman (and tier representatives) know how to vote on any particular piece of legislation. He should be required to vote with the majority if at least eight or nine of the jurors vote together. Anything less than this, then the bylaws may state that the congressman is free to vote his conscience, or must abstain. Abstaining from voting may be far less controversial and a better choice for your jury group. The bylaws requiring your congressman to vote a certain way depending on the outcome of the jury vote also eliminate the possibility that the minority may use the *Rejection Rule* as a weapon. Rejection should rarely be used for anything other than poor performance and biased representation.

What is the Rejection Rule?

The Rejection Rule is further discussed in Step 8, but here is a brief summary. *This rule allows a minority vote to remove a representative that is not meeting their expectations.* In other words, if your bylaws specifically say that the representative will only vote with the jury on an issue if the jury has at least a 9 to 3 majority and the representative voted instead with a 7 to 5 majority, then the minority can reject the representative for not following the bylaws, even though the majority may not be in favor of rejecting the representative because they got their way on an issue. This is the "checks and balance" power of the minority. A jury group must have consensus between all sides. The effort here is for all sides to be united on an issue, not just gain a slight edge that motivates the losing side to continue to argue and resent the decision of the majority.

Call your congressman's opponent or opponents to a meeting to discuss the issues, the jury group's expectations of their representative and the potentially large campaign support that will be created to help them if the candidate gets their support. Those opponents who come to your meetings may get your support; those who do not, definitely don't. Now go to Step 7.

Step 7.

Select the opponent that best represents your group, if one exists. Remember, it is very important to avoid the liberal and conservative lightning-rod issues. Those issues really do not matter—it's the system of government that matters. Good governance is what we need. This opponent can run as a Democrat or Republican, or they may run as an independent or even as a member of the Jury Party—it does not matter.

Step 8.

Get the person you selected to support for Congress to take and sign the following oath of office (This, or a similar oath, should be a requirement for all Jury Party members selected to be on a jury):

The Jury Party Oath of Office

> I do solemnly swear to uphold the will of the people and follow the bylaws of this (Jury Party 3rd tier, 2nd tier, 1st tier) and will, to the best of my ability, confer with the people of this (Jury Party 3rd tier, 2nd tier, 1st tier) on any and all issues that are important to the people I represent. In the event that one-third of the members of the (3rd tier, 2nd tier, 1st tier) jury decide, for any reason, that I should not continue with my duties, I will immediately step down from the position given me by the people of the (3rd tier, 2nd tier, 1st tier) of the Jury Party.

This is an exciting moment—now go out and celebrate! Then get the vote out and become very active in supporting your candidate so he or she does not have to get the support and finances of the special interests. That person will be YOUR representative, not the special interests'.

The hope here is that if you select a Republican or Democrat before the primary elections, then a small number of people can have a significant impact. There will be more discussion about this later.

Let's get realistic for a moment. It is not very likely that a Republican or Democratic candidate will take this oath simply because the Jury Party does not represent all of his constituents in the district. He will have some level of loyalty, particularly if you have helped his cause with a large campaign support effort. But there are limits and you will need to make a judgment call as to whether or not you will support a candidate from the two major parties. That candidate must at a minimum not be a member of a special interest organization such as ALEC. He must not accept campaign donations from outside the district and he, or a member of his staff, must promise to attend, by internet or conference call, a weekly or bi-weekly meeting of the Jury Party. And he should forward to you legislation that is pending before Congress with enough time for you to set up your Project Juries to study the legislation. You should not expect the representative to always vote your way—he has other constituents to think about. I think this would be a significant improvement over the current system and more than adequate until the Jury Party runs its own candidates for office under stricter guidelines.

Step 9.

Let's say that no candidate is acceptable to your group. It is time to select one from amongst you. Go back to the 1st tier, form groups to select potential candidates. They may be well-informed members who have impressed you, or someone outside the group.

Now a word about why I am proposing the Rejection Rule. We the people need to be cognizant of the minority. You may live in a very liberal community, but that does not give the liberals the right to walk all over and offend the conservative minority. The Rejection Rule is provided so the hard-headed conservatives and liberals do not stand a chance of pushing their agenda on you. It is also there to make sure the representatives actually do their job and not just report biased information they learn about in office. This should also alleviate fears that the candidate is too far to the left or right, not responsive to your jury group's particular philosophical beliefs, or is just a popular guy that is able to smooth talk the majority. Get the person who will provide the best representation regardless of their leanings. Also consider whether the rejection vote should be implemented with a vote of 3 or 4 jurors in a 12 man jury. One-third sounds high enough and one-quarter sounds low enough.

You may decide that the Rejection Rule is unnecessary due to the thoroughness of your bylaws. This may be true. But one day, if the bylaws are tampered with, the Rejection Rule may be your only recourse.

Here is another reason why the Rejection Rule is so important. What harm can the special interest funding of political parties and candidates, high-priced speaker fees, all-expense-paid junkets, bribes, blackmail and even threats against their life be if the people quickly respond "we told you how to vote" and yank their representative right out of office within days? Bingo! Clean government—guaranteed—for the first time in history. If the representative does not resign when told to, then the Jury Party will have to wait for the next election. Since the Jury Party was such an important part of getting this person elected, it almost guarantees that they will lose the next election. There is also the possibility of filing a recall—more on this later.

Step 10.

Select a candidate from your 1st tier group (or spokesperson for someone outside your group) that best represents your group's interests and can be responsive to your needs. He/she may even be a state legislator or local city or county commissioner who is not a member of the group. The person can also be a member of one of the tier juries who is a die-hard Republican or Democrat, but willing to live up to the oath and bylaws of your tier.

What are the ideal qualities of the person you select? Let's list them:

- This person should be someone who can figure things out.

- He/she should be a person who can report back to you the inner workings of Washington.

- This person should not be the best person who represents your conservative or liberal views, but a person who can inform you of what any legislation before Congress will mean to you and the country and, most important, who benefits.

- Should have the ability to work with all beliefs along the political spectrum.

- Should have the ability to find reliable sources of information.

- Should have the tenacity to find the truth.

- Should be open to alternative solutions.

- Should have excellent communication skills, both verbal and written.
- Should have willingness to live up to your bylaws.
- Should have the ability to "follow the money" on conflicts.
- Should possess good overall knowledge and the ability to know and find out things (verifiable) that others do not.
- Should not show obvious bias during a tense liberal vs. conservative issue.
- Should be focused on the issues that concern the people of the district.
- Has gained a high degree of trust among his/her fellow jurors.

Also remember that this representative will be making decisions quickly in the event of a crisis. They may not have time to discuss urgent matters with their peers back home or it may be of a "top secret" nature. You must select a person whose judgments you trust in an emergency or crisis, like 9/11 or Katrina, when there is no time for consultations with the jury back home.

Step 11.

Now your candidate, or candidate's spokesperson, must show up for debates and/or interviews in the 2nd tier. Facilitators play an important role here just like you see in presidential debates. They select the subject matter, number of debates and duration. Questions come from the audience, or lists of questions from the 1st and 2nd tier groups are consolidated and asked by the facilitators.

Focus the questions not on ideology, but on the candidate's character with respect to their approach to the job, experience on issues, research on issues, management of the office and the system of government. Observe the answers carefully. Are the answers phony or are the answers insightful, divulging knowledge that you were unaware of? Do not ask "are you in favor of (insert issue)" type questions. Who cares if they are? The point is that they will vote according to your party members' judgments, not theirs. They are there to faithfully represent the members of the Jury Party.

Keep in mind that we are *not* looking for the best candidate who can win the election or the person you agree with on certain issues. The person we should be looking for is knowledgeable about current events, open to other ideas, has a good eye on the real problems with government, is able to smooth over differences within the tier, and is a loyal representative of the people—not someone who wants to push their own agenda. As a member of the Jury Party, this person may have divulged verifiable evidence on issues that surprised many people. Pay particular attention to someone who knows a lot but easily says "I don't know" on some questions. It shows some honesty and this person will probably be more than willing to learn, or take the people's opinion on these issues to Washington. Watch out for the people who do not answer questions directly and who smooth talk or denigrate the audience or their opponents; these are bad people and Congress is full of them. The candidates should never be hostile in any way toward each other; this is a cooperative effort.

Remember also that during the 2nd-tier debates, candidates do not have to make the other guy look bad or dazzle the majority. They are only trying to get their name in the pot for random selection and NOT offend a potential minority that could reject them later. It's a whole different ballgame here.

Step 12.

Vote for your best candidate in the 2nd tier. If there are several excellent candidates that get a sizable vote, randomly select from that group or forward more than one.

Step 13.

Now it will be the 3rd and final tier's turn. How you go about this is up to you, but there may be follow-up debates, interviews or questions that need further inquiry. However it is handled, the 3rd tier votes for the best candidates for Congress and uses random selection to select from the field of acceptable candidates. Spokespersons for outside candidates that have lasted this far should be replaced by the candidates themselves, if they actually want to be selected.

Step 14.

The winner of the 3rd-tier election takes the oath in step 8. Now get out the vote and support your candidate with time and donations. Remember to spread the word about the Jury Party to everyone you meet. Good luck!

Campaign support is very important. It doesn't take much time or cost to distribute flyers in your neighborhood or stick a sign in your front yard. Have discussions with neighbors, coworkers, friends, places of worship, social groups, etc.

Step 15A.

You lost the election! Now what? Continue with what you are doing. Prepare for the next election. Keep putting pressure on your elected officials and become a strong supporting force for the people in your area and their grievances with the government. Be a voice for the people who get results. Build a reputation. Hopefully by this time the website will provide the necessary pamphlets and short courses on how to do all this simply and effectively. Go to step 16.

Step 15B.

You won the election! Now what? The Jury Party now works closely with the representative we send to Congress. The congressman is a regular speaker at the 3rd, 2nd, and 1st tier meetings, typically via the internet or a conference call on speaker phone. He/she is the spy who lets you know what is going on in Washington. This person will keep you informed of their conflicts, party politics and upcoming legislation that is important to you and will take questions and comments from the people back home.

You may do this for two hours a week at a regularly scheduled weekly meeting, or listen in at home via the internet and email your questions and comments. Sometimes you may talk to a staffer who is focused on a particular piece of legislation that requires detailed analysis by a Project Jury. Your representative should be able to tell you who the special interests are that support or oppose the legislation, and why.

They should be able to answer the question "Who benefits?" They may talk about a good bill before Congress that they recommend, but because of the other non-relevant legislation attached to this bill so certain legislators would support it, the representative may recommend voting against it and get your feedback on what to do. These meetings will not typically be defensive in nature where the representative has to defend their voting record, but will be constructive and positive experiences.

This is great stuff that gives you a significant insight into Washington. You will have a very constructive relationship with your representative if you break up into project groups to analyze important upcoming legislation so you can discuss the issue directly with your representative. This knowledge allows you to be truly able to talk shop with your representative and her staff to give advice, or tell your rep how to vote. You will effectively become your representative's management team.

If this is a primary victory by a Democrat or Republican candidate who was sponsored by the Jury Party, then the Jury Party gets some attention and credit for its accomplishments. The flyers sent out for the primary election show the voters that the Jury Party has credibility, especially if this was an upset victory (our candidate beat someone who was expected to win). The Jury Party should gain significant attention from this outcome. Be sure the spokespersons for the Jury Party are well versed and prepared to speak to groups or the media.

Step 16.

There are still many issues to discuss, generally and in detail, so the process continues. Discoveries are made, ideas are presented and promoted. Suddenly, due to your success, people with ideas to share, local scientists, farmers, activists, medical experts, business owners and others come to the groups to discuss issues that may be vital to the community and share important information. People with government agency issues now have someplace to go where they will be listened to and get the support they need. This party can grow to become the single best method of reaching the right people in government who can make a difference in people's lives.

Step 17.

Use the experience and knowledge gained in steps 1-16 to prepare for the next election for the offices held by local officials, state representative and senator selections, federal senator selection and even the governor and state cabinet positions. Use this method in recommending to the governor judge appointees to the various courts. Study the effects of state constitutional amendments and make informed recommendations. The list is endless of what this system can provide for your community.

New Jury Selection

It is also time to rotate a new jury. This will probably be done annually. Logically, half of the jury should be selected each year for a two-year term and one senior juror will be promoted to the next tier for a two-year term. This allows half the jury to have at least one year experience to quickly bring the new jurors up to speed on the process and the new jurors have one year of experience working with the existing jurors to decide who the best ones for promotion to the next tier are.

Chapter 8 — Ideas and Suggestions for Implementing the Jury Party

> I have as much authority as the Pope. I just don't have as many people who believe it. —*GEORGE CARLIN*

> It does not take the majority to prevail, but rather an irate, tireless minority, keen on setting brushfires of freedom in the minds of men. —*SAMUEL ADAMS*

> You have your way, I have my way. As for the right way, the correct way, and the only way, it does not exist. —*FRIEDRICH NIETZSCHE*

The structure of the Jury Party that I envision is pretty simple. The 1st tier zip code groups are where most people will participate. From the 1st tier there are paths to each elected office holder and most Project Juries will be formed from this 1st tier. Project juries will move up the tier to the state level on state issues, consolidating the opinions of other groups along the way to testify their findings and opinions. Anyone who joins the Jury Party should have a complete understanding of the organization after just two or three meetings. If not, then it's too complicated and needs modification.

Every community in the country needs to find its own passions and figure out its own solutions to problems. For those communities that seem to fail at such efforts, volunteers, a very strong characteristic of America, could surely be provided by successful communities to help show failed communities how to recover. They would not do the work for them—those days are nearly done—but show them the way to *their* version of success so that the failed community can develop their own ways to succeed. The Jury Party can be the organizer for this effort, and, through our elected officials, ensure that the government does not get in the people's way, but actually becomes a reliable working partner with the people. Governments do not ever like to lose authority—only the Jury Party can make that happen.

The number of potential campaign supporters can be significant. Just one percent of the voter population can be well over 2,000 people in any congressional district, and a significant number of these should be inspired and motivated to provide tireless efforts to get their nominee to win the election. This is actually a very large number of campaign supporters spread throughout the district that can play a very important role in the election. There are approximately 250,000 households in a typical congressional district. Just 1% of the voter population can reach every household in the district over about four Saturdays. A single person in a car can distribute dozens of flyers into mailboxes in a few hours. These flyers should include proposed projects that attract the attention of non-members or non-participating members who have a deep interest in the issue. Getting interested people involved on issues that get positive results is the main focus of the Jury Party.

Additionally, this one percent will be discussing the advantages of this system to everyone they meet, encouraging all voters—independents, Republicans and Democrats—to join and participate in a political system where the people hold responsible authority. There may also be a great deal of attention given this movement due to it being a new, unique, up-and-coming party. People will ask questions and many will learn what it is all about. One percent could become five or ten percent very quickly. A ten percent swing vote would determine many, if not most outcomes in state and federal house districts. Remember, you can virtually ignore party affiliation at this point. It won't matter what party your representative belongs to because they report to you.

Victory may not be assured, but the efforts will most certainly have an impact. The media and politicians will certainly take notice. And remember that this system, as an organization that is apolitical and beyond reproach, cannot be easily criticized. If they do, then they criticize every voter in the district. You cannot criticize its positions without criticizing the will of the people at the same time. This system may very well be difficult to attack by established politicians and institutions. Any criticism could easily backfire.

Many politicians are guilty of accepting free trips and extravagant speaker fees, and many have significantly increased their personal wealth during their time in office. All of this is powerful ammunition against incumbents—use it! This is what the people are sick and tired of. When the people hear about this system, where they create and vote for government policy and their representative becomes their

Washington contact instead of their ruler, they will begin to see the advantages of this system and vote accordingly. The members of the Jury Party will know all the dirt because they investigated the rumors and accusations to find the truth. They will speak to voters with knowledge, confidence, and authority, building a reputation that gets others involved or interested in following the Jury Party's recommendations.

The above example of selecting our representatives can easily be applied to government agencies as well. In fact, it may even be more effective. The 1st tier groups may have issues with some government agency overstepping their boundaries that political representatives can't or won't control. Through a statewide website, these issues will come to the forefront and interest throughout the state on some issues will become evident. You can form local Project Juries, coordinated statewide, that look at these issues and government agencies. Depending on the amount of interest raised, form the tier levels required to get a state-level jury that petitions the state or federal agency that governs the issue. A united effort may bring the issue to a head and the agency may be required to back off or change a regulation. The state legislature may also take notice and legislation may be proposed. If these paths do not meet your expectations, then an amendment to the state constitution may be in order. The Jury Party may become the easiest and least costly option to get an amendment on the ballot and provide an army of supporters to campaign for its passage.

Think of all the people you will meet and associate with who share common passions with you. You may find that people of different backgrounds, culture and political leanings actually agree and support you on an issue. It melts away the bias and forms bonds. You joke about each other's uniqueness and differences. You actually become friends with a common concern for government but who agree to disagree on the side issues. This could become your primary social network that greatly expands your world and relaxes your fears and insecurity around others who are different than you.

Politics can be fun. There may be intense rivalries in some meetings between the liberals and the conservatives or other opposing groups. Imagine each side voicing what they heard the night before on CNN and Fox and tossing verbal accusations and one-liners at each other—serious entertainment! The moderates of the group may come to the conclusion that both sides are kooks and look for other answers. Keep it light and humorous. That gets people to listen, participate, open their minds and keep coming back. Bull-headedness without humor turns people off. If you see the humor in these philosophical debates, share it and keep people laughing. Some members may have a keen common sense wit about them that can neutralize a heated debate. Be sure your group allows these people to talk and express their insights during discussions.

Many of us have good ideas and desires for our country mixed with misunderstandings, poor knowledge and bias. As we discuss issues with our neighbors, the bias will melt away, our knowledge will dramatically increase, and we will become focused and stronger in our core beliefs. We will gain confidence when discussing our policies and become a part of a united force on those issues we can agree on and agree to disagree on the issues we can't. We will explore and delve into our passions. This is all good stuff.

Primary Elections

Primaries may be the two mainstream parties' Achilles heel and are vulnerable to the Jury Party because of traditionally low voter turnouts in primary elections. This is where the Jury Party can have a great deal of influence early by multiplying the impact of our votes.

Let's look at the numbers. Approximately 200 million, or two-thirds of the population, are potential eligible voters. The average congressional seat therefore has 200 million divided by 435 equals about 460,000 eligible voters in each congressional district. If the Jury Party efforts can influence only 5% of eligible voters, that will be a 23,000 vote block. If the Jury Party selects a Democrat or Republican to represent them before the primary election, the Jury Party has a swing vote of 23,000 votes. Everyone in the Jury Party for this congressional seat simply switches to their candidate's party (if required by state law) so they can vote for them in the primary.

A 23,000 vote block in the 2012 primaries could have changed the outcome of 13 primary congressional races in Florida (nine of 15 contested in 2014); seven races in Pennsylvania (eight of nine contested in 2014); 33 of the 53 races in California (33 of 47 contested in 2014); 15 races in Illinois (nine of ten contested in 2014); 13 races in North Carolina (13 of 15 contested in 2014); four of the five districts in Oregon (three of five contested in 2014); and 10 of the 14 districts in Michigan (nine of 15 contested in 2014). It's clear: a 5% vote block can have significant influence on the elections of our representatives and should be an important goal for the Jury Party.

Project Juries or Committees

An important exercise is to break up into committees that discuss various issues with the intention of creating a voter guide for the next election, writing legislation to pass into law, filing an opinion paper with our representatives, doing research on specific issues or the behavior and voting records of your representatives. This can be a simple process consisting of brainstorming a list of issues that are important to everyone, listing them on paper and including a place for people's names. Add checkboxes next to the issues so people can check off those issues important to them. Then, through random selection, pick a number of interested members to be on the committee for each issue that has received sufficient numbers to be taken up. Project juries can also be requested by your elected representative or your Jury Party representative in a higher tier level. The number of jurors on a Project Jury should be no more than half of the number of interested and active members.

Discuss in your committees the issue at hand with the intention to bring all sides together rather than "winning" the argument or discussion. Trying to win the argument creates losers who will want to continue the fight for their cause with the hope of winning by eventually wearing out the opposition. Instead, use compromise and understanding to come to some resolution that all the members can live with. A great deal of internet and other research time may be needed on each issue, so do not volunteer unless you are willing to spend the required time.

Everyone needs to be understanding about opposing views and creative in bringing both sides together. From these discussions, a policy will arise that seems palatable, if not unanimously liked, by almost everyone. With thorough investigations from a wide variety of sources, the truth comes out or a significant doubt in the assumed truth becomes apparent. These Project Juries should be open forums where everyone not chosen for the jury is also welcome to participate. However, only the jury members can approve the final policy paper according to the bylaws written for this jury group. The job of the jurors is to break down the issue into manageable parts and create study groups for each part. The results of the study are reviewed and voted on for acceptance by the study group and then the jurors. The Project Jury has completed its task when all issues have been researched and voted on. Then the Project Jury reports to the organizational jury that authorized the study. If the results are divided, then both sides of the issue are discussed and how to move forward is debated.

Next it will be time to seek out other project groups in your state or federal district so you can compare notes and modify and combine the statements in the joint policy paper. Eventually you will gain statewide approval among the various Jury Party groups and you will forward the policy paper, using your representatives to formalize and introduce the legislation in the state house, if necessary. If this turns into a national policy initiative, then the state committees will have to join together to hammer out the federal legislation.

Here is an example of what a Project Jury might discuss: How thick should the asphalt be when resurfacing roads? A contractor who repaved my driveway some years ago complained that the state specification required only two inches of asphalt for road repaving projects. He argued that three inches would last twice as long and save a lot of money over the long run. The state specification was probably dictated by bureaucrats who wished to save budgets and get as many roads paved as possible (in as many legislative districts as possible). They wanted to increase the numbers—the number of miles paved—to satisfy the legislators.

Now, the effort for this contractor to change the DOT (Department of Transportation) specification on repaving in our current system would include lobbyists, lawyers, and countless hours in the state capital and DOT offices and probably some significant campaign donations. His opposition might be road contractors and the asphalt industry that see their business declining due to this effort. In other words, nothing will change in our current system. This is why people become cynical of government—it's too difficult to make simple and effective changes by knowledgeable, concerned citizens who have the skills to make improvements in the day-to-day running of the government.

However, if this was reviewed by a Project Jury, say the DOT jury, I think the people would choose quality over quantity, just as this contractor would have chosen. He is an expert in the field and a typical person who would make proposals to the jury. The county jury would promote the idea to the state regional jury, who might call in state DOT engineers (not necessarily the bureaucrats) to verify the idea, and then promote this policy to the state jury. The state jury would order its representatives in the house, or the DOT directly, to change the specification or order test roads immediately.

What also might happen in this situation is that the engineers from the DOT may bring previously completed studies that clearly show the two-inch thickness specification was, in fact, the most cost-effective solution. This revelation would instill confidence in the American people that, yes, we do have areas of good governance. Government is doing its job in many cases. It also confirms the benefits of involvement in the Jury Party—gaining knowledge of what is really going on, the good and the bad. It positively shows the benefits of creating lines of communication between government workers (not bureaucrats) and the people. It can identify the areas that are in the greatest need of public attention and also identify those areas that are operating effectively with little need for oversight.

And remember, the people who are on these committees must be in constant contact with the Jury Party members who put them there—no more secrecy and isolation can be tolerated.

Another very important example of the Project Jury is to actually execute a program. I am referring to local programs for a city, county or group of counties that are driven to solve a problem. These problems may be charitable in nature, such as helping the homeless get back on their feet, building local farmers markets, opening up health clinics, building better race relations, lowering the divorce rate, dealing with abandoned buildings, etc. These Project Juries may be the most important efforts of the Jury Party and will create excellent public relations. And when these kinds of passionate efforts work closely with existing charities, government agencies, businesses and other organizations, I believe your community can be transformed over a period of a few short years. When the people and institutions merge together with a common goal, amazing things can happen.

Bridge Juries

Bridge juries can be used when a jury is hopelessly split on an issue. Randomly select twelve jurors from the next lower level tier of the tier with the problem deciding on the issue. Give the bridge jurors the job of finding common ground and "bridging the gap" between the divided groups. Emphasize that the bridge jury is not there to decide which side is right, but to delve deeper into the subject and come up with a better solution that all sides can be satisfied with. Sometimes the jury might need a new group of outsiders to take a fresh look at an issue to come up with a better solution or decide an issue with additional investigation. The bridge jury will ask questions and do additional research that is focused on satisfying all sides of the issue.

Zip Codes

This system is initially based on zip codes, because this is thought to be the simplest starting point to organize the party. Population densities vary widely within zip codes, from tens of thousands to just a few individuals. So, the state or congressional level group needs to address this organizational issue to come up with potential alternatives, such as using entire counties for rural communities, and creating one or two lower tiers below the existing 1st tier in highly populated and active zip codes, depending on the number of participants. Or perhaps there could be a county-based system. If a congressional district Jury Party group is having difficulty recruiting enough members to start groups within the zip codes, then a congressional district group should be formed first.

Congressional Districts

This system might become a typical third party of about three or four hundred thousand members initially. Growth is important to compete with the two main parties, so how do we break away from the typical third party membership numbers? Let's do the math.

Initially the Jury Party membership may stabilize at about 1,000 members per congressional district. Each district can develop a one-page flyer that describes who we are and what we are working on. Include possible discoveries about your representatives or focus on local issues or legislation that is getting a lot of current attention. Assuming color printed flyers, the cost to distribute these flyers is about 7 cents each (paper is cheap, but ink is not). So, for each member, a donation of $3.50 a week can reach 50 households, or 5,000 households for the congressional district. There are about 250,000 households in a typical congressional district, so in 50 weeks, or one year, the Jury Party has reached every single household in the country. If just one per cent of the people show an interest in the Jury Party as a result of the flyer, that raises our membership by about 2 million members nationally and, just like that, the Jury Party is, by far, the most dominant third party in the country. Now, with 2.5 million members, each member can donate $3.50 a month and reach every household in America with a monthly newsletter. There is no way to predict what will happen then. Some districts will have more success than others with eye-catching flyers that can be shared with all groups to improve on promoting the Jury Party's efforts.

State Level Notes

For a state level, there can now be an agenda promoting the interests of the jury members on state-wide issues. Lower levels highlight their most pressing issues that concern them and forward their ideas for solutions to the state level. The state party should have a bit more pull to get outsiders involved such as state officials or experts in the appropriate fields of interest. The state level jury should study and air all sides of an issue, and form debates so that people have the ability to challenge the authorities on their statements. Once these issues are settled and real solutions are developed, these solutions are added to the Jury Party state platform. A party platform represents the agenda of the members of that state and provides goals that the statewide system can shoot for, rather than just putting out the useless electioneering that the two-party platforms typically reflect. Also, these state platforms should be oriented much more toward local or state issues and not just reflect the national agenda of the party.

National Level Notes

Once the state jury parties are firmly established and effective methods are developed for handling issues, then it will be time to go regional. Break the country up into six sections of 7-10 states depending on geographic location and population, then progress to the national level in a similar way as you did on the state level.

The national chairman, and perhaps a co-chairman, may be able to get themselves invited to a great many media outlets to express the Jury Party agenda. They can list many examples of instances in which the agenda items have already had significant success in state and local districts. It can be a powerful influence on the mainstream to have a knowledgeable and influential Jury Party leadership team on the national level.

The national level, national regional level and perhaps the state level jury members may need to be paid for their services as well as maintain some administrative staff. We will have to figure out a way to get funding that does not influence the members' actions or opinions. Once the party goes national, I intend to turn my website over to a national committee.

What about the White House? Let's not get ahead of ourselves. We are a very long way from that. Former Speaker of the House Tip O'Neal was often quoted as saying "all politics is local." Is the reason that third parties are so unsuccessful that they focus on running for President before they have a strong base of support? The Jury Party described in this book is all about local. Getting local organizations involved with government agencies and locally elected officials is what this party needs to focus on first. The office of the President can come later after a minimum of local and state governments are successfully led by the Jury Party. This party needs to establish itself in local areas, then at the state and congressional levels—not by immediately jumping into hopeless efforts for the White House, as other third parties do. We need to build a base first. I would like to see 100 members of Congress and about 20 senators elected from the

Jury Party before we consider a run for the White House. Let's get a few governors and the majority of a dozen state legislators as well.

Funding the Party and Projects

How do we fund this party without allowing influence? First, let's look at how we can get funding and then we can look at where it goes and how to manage it.

One way to get funding is to set up or hire an organization that does not have any contacts with the Jury Party. This could be an accounting firm. A person who wishes to donate $100 to the party's organization efforts would go to the website set up by the accounting firm and enter the amount and where that person wants the money to go. For example, the person may want half the money to go to his zip code group because of a major project that they are getting started in, then 20% to the state and 30% to the national party to help pay for staff and travel expenses. If there are national party advertising funds, then the person may give a percentage to that fund to help the national party advertise during a campaign season or to promote the party itself. During campaigns people who want to make donations to candidates will select which of the candidates get their donation.

All the funding is kept extremely confidential or unverifiable, except by the IRS of course. The only thing that the Jury Party entity knows about the funds is that they received a sum this week from one or more anonymous donors. This method does not stop a large donor from saying to a jury that if they do what the donor wants they will get the money. Well, the whole point of the Jury Party is that I trust that my friends, neighbors and co-workers will not accept a bribe and I also trust that the two main parties most definitely will. This is honest government through an honest system within a political party. No doubt that a few very difficult situations will arise and the bribes will be taken, but this cannot possibly go very far up the ladder; certainly not to the state or national level. And don't forget, half the jurors that took the bribe will be gone in less than a year when their two year term expires. Now the bribe cycle starts all over again, this time with idealistic people who are stunned at *what* has happened because they do not understand *why* it happened. The newbies will be thinking how to get out of this mess and reverse the damage. With this system, bribes and influence peddling becomes a very poor long term investment.

Where do the funds go? There will be travel expense burdens for your representatives that your jury group will feel obligated to pay for. The state and national parties will have administrative, travel and office expenses. The website may need a major upgrade and constant IT support. Your zip code group has flyer expenses such as ink, paper and printers. And during campaigns there are yard signs, bumper stickers, flyers and advertising costs for newspaper, TV and radio.

How do we manage these funds? Advertising should be handled by Project Juries that manage the advertising campaign effort. This effort may be theme based or a temporary ad blitz. Election advertising should be handled by a Project Jury associated with the campaign staff from the district or state. State and national administrative expenses should be managed by the Jury Party organization as described in the previous chapter. There should not be ads extolling the virtues of the Jury Party candidate for office because people are not voting for the candidate, they are voting for the Jury Party members who control their candidate while in office. People will vote according to the policies established by the Jury Party for the candidate's district or state. And yes, there will be negative advertising because of the Jury Party's investigations into their opponents' list of campaign donations from outside their district, memberships in special interest organizations, all-expense-paid junkets, exorbitant speaker fees and how their voting record reflects all this influence. If our communication methods are effective, things will most definitely change.

More on Lightning-Rod Issues

An example of a lightning-rod issue was the George Zimmerman trial. George Zimmerman was charged with murder in the second degree of Trayvon Martin. We the people may never know the truth in this case, as the governor said, "the people have to trust the system." Wrong, Governor! The people do *not* "have to trust the system." The people have to get *involved* in the system.

A local Jury Party group as described above can form a Project Jury to be a grand jury of sorts that would investigate these kinds of instances and judge if the police procedures were correctly followed. Therefore, if the police did do their job correctly according to law, then the jury exonerates them in front of the media and calms everyone down. The police are able to go about their business as usual without a stigma attached that has been blown up by the media who are just trying to get the attention they need in order to sell advertising and advance careers. If the police or District

Attorney's Office did not follow proper procedures, then the individual(s) are disciplined in an appropriate manner, justice is served and the cloud over the other police officers in the department will eventually fade because the "bad apples" have been dealt with.

Will the jury type system quell the emotions generated by community leaders and magnified by the media over such events? Only after the Jury Party can earn the support and trust of much of the population in every community, and after years of proven success at mundane issues that the people benefit from, will these events become efforts at improving law versus cultural battles. Time will tell, but the current system is generating a great deal of distrust and animosity that appears to have no end in sight and may be getting worse.

Also, another jury can be set up to judge whether the so called "stand-your-ground" laws are appropriately written or followed. Currently, the state legislatures are under pressure to revoke these self-defense laws and this will no doubt become a campaign issue. Do you think the legislators will consciously review these laws for flaws and fix them with honesty and integrity? How can they? And how can the people tell the legislators what to do if the people do not know what really happened and how it happened. Can you imagine a state legislator who supports these laws offering to sit down with the opposition to discuss whether they are valid or not? It will never happen with the current divisions between the two parties. Legislators cannot and will not show any weakness to their opposition.

I'm sure many legislators are considering the reelection liabilities of their decision. They will not consider what is right, they will only think where they need to stand to get reelected; they may just follow their party line and be trained by their party to respond to attacks with the usual one-liners. The Jury Party removes this flaw from the system and places the people in the position to reverse, keep, change or fix the law. The people, through the Jury Party, tell the legislators what to do, and they do it—or else!

I am sure that these juries may not return a unanimous verdict on these issues, but may return a large majority. Each side can voice their reasons why they support one side over the other, just like Supreme Court decisions, to let the people judge their logic. The important thing here is that the people get a crack at fixing the system the way they deem necessary, not because it is politically expedient, but because they believe in what they are doing and they must, themselves, live under their decisions.

A more recent major issue is the Ferguson, Missouri killing of an eighteen year old youth by a police officer—another case where the people may never know what really happened. What is disturbing about this case to me is the reaction to the grand jury decision. I believe that the grand jury system is, by far, the fairest system in history and should not be tampered with carelessly. If the people do not trust the grand jury, then they might eventually insist on a new system that will most definitely be worse, at least long term.

These kinds of conflicts provide the justification that some powerful leaders use to tamper with the rights of the people, all in the name of justice. An important aspect of the Jury Party will be to inform the American people of the origins and value of the jury system, why it exists and is such an essential part of our freedoms. Perhaps improvements in the current judicial jury system are necessary, but the essential characteristic of a "random jury of peers" is essential to maintain.

If your jury is compelled to discuss these emotional issues early in its development, then keep in mind that if discussions get out of hand and people start leaving the organization, the benefits simply will not be there. But if you are successful, then by all means continue these discussions. Your positive experience will be invaluable to the juries that may have trouble with this effort.

Stories

Everybody has a story to tell. Sharing stories with each other will spark an idea or identify a subject that requires investigation. People will give examples of how unfair a law may be, their experience of corruption in government or an example of where government was very successful at solving their problem. These stories need to be shared with other people—they are the people's experience with government or our society—the good and the bad. It will help to identify the weaknesses in the system that need immediate attention. Our system is not broken, but the system can clearly be run better (and probably a whole lot cheaper), and the stories of our experiences can identify many of the problems that should be tackled first.

Listeners vs. Talkers

I believe the Jury Party is primarily for listeners, not talkers. We need more listeners making the decisions in our communities and country. We need people whose beliefs are not engraved in stone with one-liners but who believe that the path to truth and understanding requires listening, research and contemplation, followed with expressions of original thought. It's better to sleep on an idea versus using rehearsed philosophical comebacks that do not address the opponent's issues.

This should be commonly seen in Project Juries. The next morning after a meeting there may be an explosion of emails to fellow jurors with thoughts and evidence about what was discovered or discussed the night before.

Volunteerism

When this system is in solid standing with your community, or even before, volunteerism will be a key aspect of the Jury Party. In order to take back America, you have to take control of your community. The Jury Party can be a major focal point for volunteer organizations and working charities (such as Habitat for Humanity). Imagine this: a charity requires assistance from the community, so the Jury Party provides access to literally thousands of potential volunteers who have a passion and sense of duty for their community. Many people have a desire to volunteer, but simply have no place to go that fits their interests. The Jury Party can be that place.

Local Programs

Another focus is to try to find local alternatives to federal programs. Federal programs mean federal control over your community. Local control means more of a hands-on approach that can be much more effective at solving problems with little cost. Elected officials and bureaucrats actively pursue federal grants because they have to say they are doing everything possible to improve a situation, whether helpful or not. The local community needs to review these grants to see if they are really worthwhile for the community and are not used as a sales pitch in an election campaign.

Random Representation

Why should there be random selection of the tier representatives? I believe if the selection of our representatives were done strictly by vote, then many people who are very well qualified to lead would never be given the opportunity. Also, random representation filters out the egotistical, misguided, charismatic personalities and philosophical agendas that dominate these kinds of organizations. People will lie and hide their true agendas in order to get elected, so strictly utilizing the election of representatives rather than random selection will eventually alienate many of the members. This is exactly what seems to be happening with our current political system. Also, when someone wins a vote, it may affect their ego; some may believe they have been given a mandate to do whatever they want. Random selection removes the "anointed" mentality and the idea of a "debt" owed to their supporters that exists with current representatives.

People get involved if one day they may be selected as a juror and have a voice for their opinions. Some people who are capable of leading too often have quiet lives until one day they have experiences that give them the confidence to speak and argue. Random representation also lowers people's expectations of fellow jurors and tier members. New representatives are not "on the spot" to perform immediately and existing jurors offer support to the new ones because they were in the same position before and the newbie is not seen as a threat. These factors make this system a cooperative one, not a competitive one.

Random selection will bring many different people of a wide variety of backgrounds to the table, which should create some lively debates filled with new insights into issues.

Look at the justice system's use of randomly selected juries. If you are wrongly accused of murder, you must convince a jury, randomly selected, of your innocence. This jury is made up of people from a wide variety of backgrounds and demographics. They know little to nothing about criminal investigations, DNA testing and forensics. And yet the jury system, which was officially instituted some 800 years ago by the Magna Carta, is still with us today. Would you give up your right to be judged by a jury of your peers? Hardly anyone would. The people trust random selection, so let's expand it for the selection of our leaders and the running of our government.

The first democracies in ancient Greece used random selection to pick their leaders and this form of government survived in some city-states for up to a thousand years until they were swallowed up by empire. The Greek democracies and the 800-year-old Anglo-American jury system make random representation an already proven system of governance.

Review of Legislation

One of the most important duties of the Jury Party is to review legislation. This can be a simple and speedy process once adequate numbers of citizens join the Jury Party. Any bill before Congress can be reviewed by juries across the country. Some of these bills are massive documents that our legislators have no hope of reading, let alone understanding in detail. They have no choice but to follow the party leaders whose real agenda is unknown. We can help.

Take any bill before Congress, break it down into sections of a few pages and distribute them to various zip code juries across the country. One ten-page section may be assigned to a dozen or even a hundred zip code based Project Juries who review and summarize the section assigned. These summaries are then reviewed by the next tier, consolidating the data and research, then, they are passed onward to the state level and eventually reach a national jury committee that produces a national summary and policy statement. Conflicts between the summaries are resolved or simply noted.

The national jury summarizes the effects that the legislation will have on the country and determines what the bill actually accomplishes and who benefits. They return this summary back to the local juries, who can then decide to support or reject the bill and inform their representative how to vote. If the bill is considered a good idea overall and has only a few serious flaws that should be corrected, then this legislative review process can also advise and recommend how to change the bill so that it can be supported by the jury members.

A system of reviewing legislation can be that simple and is vitally important. Any single individual need spend only a little time reviewing their assigned section of a bill. The response rate should be pretty high and result in quick decisions, although a large bill such as the Affordable Care

Act may take a year or more of intense study before the conclusions and alternate wording of the bill is complete.

There will be obvious liberal/conservative, urban/suburban/rural, rich/poor, taxpayer/tax receiver and class conflicts on many issues. Unlike the way things have been done in the past, *these conflicts should not be fought to get a 51% majority,* but should focus instead on *alternative ideas that satisfy all sides.* Any bill that cannot get support from the *vast* majority of people is probably better off being rejected.

The Staff of Your Elected Representative

Think about this. Who are the staffers that support your state or federal representative? Why not select these persons from the Jury Party once the party's candidates start winning elections? Who says we can only send one person to Washington? Let's send a team to Washington. Write your bylaws accordingly and develop methods to allow this to happen effectively to ensure that your representative has as many eyes and ears as possible listening and watching everything that is going on in Washington to report back to the Jury Party. Why be dependent on only one person?

These staffers are capable of offering a different perspective on an issue or even being a specialist on an area of government that concerns the people of the district, such as a college professor who specializes in a field that is currently a hot topic in the state. The professor simply takes a one or two year sabbatical in Washington to delve deeper into the issue with the federal agencies or congressional committees that have authority over the issue.

K Street Becomes State Street

"K Street" refers to an actual street in downtown Washington DC that was the street address of many lobbyists, think tanks and other advocacy type groups. Many of these groups have moved to other locations but the street name is still used as a reference to the special interests in Washington.

If the Jury Party succeeds in getting congressmen and senators elected, then to that degree these special interests will not get the return on investment required to justify their expense and will abandon support for their offices. Let's replace these special interests with state offices that house the interests of the people in the state. Get your state to buy or lease these offices and convert them to dormitories or apartments that house summer student interns and co-ops, or professionals that get up close and in-depth with the federal agency or department that is involved in a current issue in your state or district. Or the students and professionals can just expand their knowledge on their field of study. Housing is very expensive in DC and such persons will need low or no-cost housing that can utilize the local mass transit system.

These offices can also house your state and district's special representatives for issues that they must work closely with Congress on. In other words, "K Street" will become "State Street," where each state maintains an office/housing building that offers low or no-cost housing for the people in your state that have an interest in Washington as well as an office that assists the efforts. State Street will be known as the people's lobby, think tank or advocacy group. These offices will allow ordinary people to get up close with the agency or department that deals with their ideas and passions. They will work and advance their skills and abilities with knowledgeable government workers, not be stonewalled by government bureaucrats. It will take maybe a month or two of a special one cent sales tax in your state to pay and maintain this effort for years. You will be investing in your federal government and replace the special interests that dominate the DC scene today. Just make sure the politicians in your state have absolutely no control over this effort whatsoever. And don't forget your state capital either. Each county or each state Senate district may have a state house/office in your capital doing the same thing as at the federal level.

A Message to all Elected Representatives

I would like to make a plea to all elected representatives to join the Jury Party. There are many reasons to do so once the Jury Party is relatively established. They are:

- A potentially very large and active group of campaign supporters
- Never again being pressured to follow the party line created by the power brokers against the will of your constituents
- Never again kissing up to donors or voting blocks
- Never again having to defend your vote to a disgruntled constituent or group since you are bound by the bylaws on how to vote

- Never again make speeches to special interest groups or expend valuable time on other efforts for campaign donations
- Never again worry about the next election
- Never again worry about how voters will react to your vote on legislation
- Always have a knowledgeable group of ardent and tenacious detectives ready to investigate anything you want or need to know
- Always have the support of your constituents—the conflict is within the constituents, not with you.

Regardless of your past voting record or party affiliation, your experience and knowledge of the inner workings of the state or federal legislature is valuable to your constituents. You are aware of how a lot of things are done in your government. You are aware of the lies and myths; you know the rights and wrongs and should be able to provide a great deal of insider information that is not generally known by the public. If you are willing to let go of your philosophical constraints, work hard, be honest, loyal and forthright, you should be a shoe-in as a Jury Party candidate regardless of your previous party affiliation or voting record.

When the Jury Party national membership passes one million, check the membership in your district or state, and if the numbers indicate an active membership you should seriously consider the Jury Party option. It could really make a difference in your career.

What Else Can the Jury Party Do?

Everything! Remember that the goal here is to create a think tank of massive proportions that, rather than being made up of agenda-driven elitists, is composed of concerned and inquisitive people who want to know what is really going on. People who are confused and distrustful of the biased arguments of the politicians, media and self-appointed experts need an organization that focuses on finding the truth.

If you are not successful in electing your representative, you can still put a great deal of pressure on her/him and others. You are now organized to send vast numbers of emails and letters to your representatives, telling them how to vote on upcoming legislation. In 18 states, there are laws permitting the recall of your Senator or Congressman. Do research to see how to recall your representative and if your state does not permit recalls, then form a committee to add this feature to your state constitution immediately. The bad publicity, or the threat of recall, may be all it takes to rattle a representative enough to fall in line with the people's desires. Amazingly, a U.S. representative has never been recalled. Make history—be the first! If it is justified, of course!

Another example is crime. How can this system lower the crime rate? Delve into the mind of an offender for just a moment. I'm not talking about a hardened criminal here; I'm talking about ordinary people. People who cheat on their taxes, people who take more fish than the state wildlife division allows, speeders, etc.

These people will be sitting on juries arguing for fewer restrictions. Some will win because they actually do have legitimate arguments, and some will lose. The difference here is that at least they were involved in the decision making process. Once a decision is made, they will not only avoid being caught by the authorities, but will also avoid being identified by the general population, some of whom were involved in making the ruling the offender is trying to break. This system will greatly add to the manpower required to police policy by adding the element of peer pressure to the equation. Offenders may look at things very differently if their actions are disapproved of by a large group of their peers who believe in the jury process of making the rules or laws that they live under. Their peers will expect everyone to live under the people's rules and laws and will have less tolerance for misbehavior than today's "beat the system" mentality, since under a jury system of government—*their peers are the system!* This system may work because they had their chance to win over their peers and they lost. But sometimes they might also win. People are much more willing to accept the people's will than the law of a government that they feel does not understand their point of view. This attitude adjustment may filter down to potential violent criminals in our society, particularly when they are young, before they commit violent acts. I think most violent criminals simply got away with too much before they became violent. The increased manpower the jury system creates in policing our streets may catch these people and persuade them to seek alternate paths. Our crime rates, for all crimes, just might plummet from where they are now.

And another issue today is privacy. The paparazzi can harass famous people that are just leaving a restaurant or even photograph them behind their walled back yard. People can record an embarrassing moment in your life and you can become a You Tube sensation overnight. New technology like Google Glass can essentially eliminate all privacy outside of our homes. The government is trying to monitor your phone calls without judicial oversight. Are these invasions of our privacy supported by the morals and ethics of the American people?

A jury started in many local communities throughout the country, and rising to the national level through a tier system, can develop the standards by which society values privacy on a local, state and national level. This policy of privacy passed by state or federal legislators into law and modified on a regular basis as ethics and technology evolves, will reflect the morals and values of the American people and should be widely accepted and adhered to. This jury can essentially become a permanent standards committee, constantly reviewing new technology and the changing values of the American people's views of privacy. Remember, the persons on the jury must live under these rules as well. They do not live under a different set of rules like Congress does. There is no profit or glory either way they vote—they are generally independent of all that.

In fact, the Jury Party can create hundreds of concurrent standards committees that develop guidelines by which society lives. A similar process is carried out throughout industry and commercial construction. There are boiler standards, piping standards, electrical standards, manufacturing quality standards and safety standards, all supported privately by energetic and committed professionals. Some of these standards are copied word-for-word into the OSHA regulations. In my 30+ years' experience as an engineer, nobody has ever suggested or even hinted at violating the National Electric Code (NEC) simply because the rules are made by the very people who are involved in the everyday business of electrical design, construction and inspection.

These standards juries, acting like private standards committees, can be a process that looks at government policy and law to review revisions to the laws based on ideas and feedback from the people discussing these issues in the lower, local tiers. From time to time they will revise the laws and forward them to state and federal legislatures for legal review and passage. The media will be used to explain and summarize the changes. The police or policing authority hands out warnings for six months or so until the people or businesses are thoroughly informed of the changes. Can you think of anything wrong with this?

Discuss the amendments to your state constitution in the upcoming election. What is the problem that caused the amendment to be created? Always ask:

- "Who benefits?"
- "What groups or special interests favor the amendment and why?"
- "What groups oppose and why?"
- And always "follow the money" on every amendment or piece of legislation.

Continue discussions until it becomes very clear what the vote decision should be. In fact, this organization makes it simple and easy to get the signatures required to put amendments on the ballot—that is, if the amendment has merit. This system could greatly influence and make a name for itself by adding and supporting amendments to state constitutions. Groups that want an amendment to the state constitution will know that the chances of success are nearly zero without the support of the Jury Party—a party whose values and morals cannot and will not be compromised.

How about conspiracy theories? There are a lot of conspiracy theories or urban legends going around today. We can investigate these theories and find out if they are justified or not. Of the over 30,000 populated zip codes in the country, there could be dozens that are doing the same thing you are. These juries need to connect with each other and compare notes. If found to be valid, we have a large and active group to push for an official investigation up to the national level of the Jury Party based on the knowledge gained by the group. The state or federal agency/department responsible for the issue will not be able to easily dismiss or ignore a small but tenacious and determined group of active citizens who are well informed and organized for the cause.

Jobs

How can an organization like the Jury Party create jobs? If your community is having a problem getting and retaining good jobs, then the Jury Party may be able to help. The Jury Party brings together many people from all walks of life that can offer ideas for products and services that are needed in the community. The party brings together a wide range of knowledge and skills that can give someone with a business idea quality guidance. A Project Jury should be set up that looks at creating jobs and small businesses, using its exceptional understanding of the skills and knowledge that exist in the community to offer assistance in the effort.

It will also be important to study how money flows in and out of your community. If the people are spending all their money on services and products that are provided from outside your community, then risk to your community's economic health is inevitable. The slightest disruption in jobs can send the community into a tailspin. Examples of money leaving the community includes taxes, electric bills, big box stores, car and truck purchases, phone bills and food. Examples of money entering a community include salaries, pensions, investment income, Social Security and locally owned production (such as farms, small manufacturing, etc.) Communities must become self-supporting to some degree so that calamities such as the shutdown of a major manufacturing plant does not have a devastating negative impact. The community will have a better focus on how to create and maintain wealth with a clear understanding of how and why money enters and leaves your community.

The community can stop money from leaving by supporting small businesses that provide the necessary products and services locally. Even a general understanding of the flow of money by the community may get people to instinctively support local restaurants that use locally grown produce and meats over a national chain. You may find out that even if you can buy it cheaper from outside the community, buying local can have a far more positive impact that results in more local wealth that you personally benefit from. You may find that the city might spend more for something provided locally, but is able to recoup the difference in more tax revenue. All this knowledge is gained through a passionate and energized group of people with a clear understanding of their mission. And the knowledge gained through their experience is disseminated throughout the community by the Jury Party or similar organization.

Use Flyers

Don't underestimate the power of flyers. I think this could be the primary communication method utilized by the party to potential members and trusting voters. A single sheet of color printed paper, costing about seven cents, describing the benefits and successes of your local jury, explaining the jury system itself, providing meeting schedules and a listing of issues currently being proposed and discussed, could have a very powerful impact. A few dozen people in one zip code can distribute these inexpensive flyers to most addresses fairly quickly. Personally, I totally ignore expensive television commercials but almost always read the flyers placed in my mailbox or left on my door, even if only briefly to check them out. They are cheap and they get to the audience you want—your neighbors.

If only one percent of households in your zip code, city, county or congressional district are members of the Jury Party, then each member would only have to drop off as few as ten flyers a night on their way home from work for two to three weeks. Every person living in your tier area would then be informed about the party, what it stands for, the benefits of membership, election recommendations, dirt on their representative and the important issues that you are discussing. If this effort is successful, your membership should increase and the distribution effort needed on your part should decline quickly. Some people may give the flyer just a cursory glance, but one day may see a proposed issue that really sparks their passion. That person may join just to get involved on the one issue. After the issue is resolve the individual may drop out, but always follow the Jury Party's advice at the voting booth because they saw what a trusted organization that the party is. These are the methods we need to develop to become a strong and viable force in our community.

In particular, flyers may be very effective during elections. The Jury Party flyer would include the party's recommendations for who to vote for or which state amendments to approve based on your tier's analysis. Each voter is given a piece of paper to take with them into the voting booth. Even people who are not members may vote according to the Jury Party recommendations because they are sick and tired of the two-party politics or they overheard a conversation in the office about what the Jury Party stands for. This could really make a difference in elections. Only one percent of households can multiply their influence many times. Donate accordingly for paper, ink and printers to make this successful.

Age

Let's talk about the advantages of the Jury Party and the generation gap. Today, Congress is made up of mostly old white guys. "Good," you may say, if you're an old white guy.

But that creates conflict and distrust between generations, sexes, races, religions and classes. Because the jury is created through random selection, anyone has as much of a chance of moving up the ladder as the old white guy. It all depends on involvement, performance, gaining respect from your peers, and luck. Older people can temper the impulsiveness of younger people and young people can jar the comfort zone of the older people. Both efforts succeed at making people think. But there should be a natural balance between stagnation and too much change. Change will require a good argument, and resisting change will require a good argument too. If too much change is occurring, older people get more involved and tip the balance. The same happens with too little change, except it's the young people who join. There is a natural balance in the jury.

Foreign Policy

How about foreign policy? Sure, why not? Submit an issue of current importance on foreign policy and set up state, regional and then national juries to set the policy of our state department based on extensive research by the members and supporters. Do conference calls and internet discussions. Set up internet conferences with authors, state department officials and even foreign officials. Be sure to talk to people who live or had lived in the subject foreign country to find out what is really going on inside. Do not trust any single source of information, but put it all together and figure out the motives of the sources.

I even envision one day having ambassador jury groups that travel to the country of their choice and involve themselves in foreign diplomacy, business development and just plain good relations. They may interact with the U.S. Ambassador on issues between our two countries and argue for a change in America's foreign policy. These ambassador juries may include immigrants or descendants from that country as well as Americans who have an interest for some reason. These juries will also report back to other jury members what is really happening in that country that our politicians and media are not reporting. And they will be spreading the jury concept worldwide!

Has the Israeli and Palestinian conflict gone on long enough? Do you honestly think that the politicians will solve the problem? The politicians have been given many decades to make the effort and the result is that the two sides are more divided today than ever. The politicians will not solve the problems until they are good and ready—if ever. This conflict can be solved when the people sit down and begin talking. Talking about the history, the conflict, the problems of living day to day, the future and the economic impact will begin the healing process. Randomly selected jury groups created with members of all sides dedicated to understanding and solving each and every issue in the conflict may be the only path to peace in that region.

Advocacy Groups

There are many advocacy groups in America that profess truths and good causes, yet these truths and causes are difficult to spread throughout the general population. The advocacy groups operate on shoestring budgets and cannot pay for the attention that they need or deserve because there is no tangible profit in their passions that financial supporters can benefit from. But the Jury Party can provide the path of recognition to a much wider and more varied audience than is otherwise possible. If their cause is just and their version of the truth is verified, then they have just added many more followers and helpers to their cause that can benefit them. The varied skills and abilities of their new

Jury Party audience also offer cost effective alternatives to the promotional methods currently used by some advocacy groups. This can help them spread their causes more efficiently and to an ever wider audience.

The intent here is to make the Jury Party the premier "go to" place for any group or organization that seeks support for a local, state or national issue or cause. By supporting such causes, and identifying those causes that do not meet the community standards, the party gains credibility, community trust and a strong reputation as a participatory organization. We don't just listen, we get involved. A small and sincere advocacy group that pleads for assistance to several thousand local party members can be very successful attracting sufficient volunteers to help out on a quick weekend project or for long-term efforts.

Party Growth

How big does the Jury Party need to be? Not all that big, in my opinion. If there are many great problems and challenges identified by the Jury Party that need attention, then ten percent of voters, or about 20 million, should be adequate. Many of the other ninety percent will just follow the Jury Party because they have seen the ideas and positive results promoted by this party and many are very sick of the two-party status quo. Once the Jury Party is firmly in place and has implemented effective change, only five percent or less may be enough to maintain good governance. If certain agendas or philosophies tend to dominate jury groups, this will get the attention of dissenters in the community and prompt them to join in. The new members can quickly tip the balance away from any dominating philosophical beliefs.

Many of the ninety or ninety-five percent who do not get involved will still learn to trust the judgments of the party because things are running so well. And anyone with a gripe is free to join the party and have immediate influence if they choose to do so and their argument is worthy.

A likely early scenario may be that the national membership of the Jury Party levels off at typical numbers for existing third parties. If this happens then the organization might be congressional district based. Say we get into the 40-50,000 range or 100 members per house district. The primary focus might begin with the structure of the local, state and national organizations.

Only after this effort would it be time to focus on the elected officials or candidates for office. Create a list of questions that you would like to ask candidates for upcoming elections to state house and senate races, federal house and senate races, local races and others pertaining to their campaign finance, free trips, speaker fees, respect of the people's will, etc. Then call each candidate or their campaign office and gather answers to your questions. Verify and summarize your notes for each candidate for each office in the upcoming election to determine if they hold up to your values and morals by avoiding the party line and the special interests.

Now get the other 200,000 + households in your federal district informed. Start first with a flyer that describes what the Jury Party is and what it stands for and what issues are on the top of your group's agenda. Follow through, possibly many months later near an election cycle, with a review of candidates and select which candidates meet or do not meet your criteria and why. Be sure to identify the sources of your negative viewpoint of any candidate and be sure the source is not their opponent. If all candidates are acceptable, then say so, and if all are not acceptable, also say so—do not choose the lesser of two evils any more. Spread these flyers to as many households as possible. With luck you will gain membership that will help in future efforts.

This would be a large effort for only 100 people but could lead to 1,000 new members quickly. Since you are already organized and structured, you are more able to absorb a large influx of members and quickly break the district up into zip code groups.

Stopping Leaders in the Jury Party Who Defy its Principles

If the wrong people rise to the top leadership positions in the Jury Party and begin to make unpopular decisions, the people have three ways of reacting that will quickly put a stop to the unwanted actions. This could happen if the Jury Party is a victim of its success—that is, people are so happy with the way things are running that they think it will last forever without their attention—it just runs by itself. Under other forms of government it may be too late at this point to fix the problems without upheaval across the land due to the central power of the government, but with a system of government that uses the principles of the Jury Party, it is very simple.

First, the people who oppose their representative's actions will join the Jury Party in droves, thereby tipping the balance of the majority. Existing representatives will quickly learn that any public attention that their actions and policies get will bring an immediate response from the public. This will become something to avoid by making sure that all sides are represented in the decision-making process.

Second, there is the Rejection Rule, which allows a minority of the jurors to reject individual leaders. I cannot more strongly emphasize my belief that this rule is critical for success in order to control your representative.

But, third, if the people tend not to use the Rejection Rule, or it is not passed as a rule in your district, then the Jury Party members will argue for the removal of the elected representative at the next election. Within the jury organization, they are simply rotated out and their climb up the ladder is halted. Your bylaws, developed for your area, should include methods for the minority to adequately express their displeasure towards a representative that only favors the majority—or else there will only be conflict.

This system of electing representatives can work much more honestly and effectively than the two-party republican system because representatives from all levels will be in constant contact with the people who put them there, and everybody will know where the campaign money is coming from because of the guidelines you have implemented in your bylaws. The majority must defend their view on an issue; they cannot ignore a vocal minority which expresses the faults of the mainstream view during a discussion, especially if the Rejection Rule is implemented. And, of course, the minority must defend their views before the majority as well. The Jury Party methods described in this book and further developed by the membership will make everybody a lot smarter and better able to express themselves and think through arguments.

The Do's

- Do join, and, if you are not inclined to speak or participate, just listen and learn. Eventually you may have a brilliant idea that makes a real difference when an issue that sparks your passion comes up for discussion.
- Do pay a great deal of attention to the bylaws of your jury. Bylaws are required to create predictable organizational procedures.
- Do create some kind of "oath of office" for each selected member of a jury. It can be as simple as a promise to just follow the bylaws developed by your jury group.
- Do check the Jury Party website from time to time to see additional helpful information. In time, I hope that there will be numerous brochures and other downloads that help the meetings progress, as well as reports and articles from various groups around the country to see what others are doing and how they have learned to succeed with their goals.
- Do believe that you and your community can make a difference. Eventually your efforts will pay off; it's just a matter of time, and this will motivate and inspire you and your group even more.
- Do use some form of random representation for the upper tiers and only use random representation for the 1st tier.
- Do support your candidates for public office with your time and donations once they are selected.

- Do listen to others and pay close attention to what they really are trying to say. We are not used to talking about politics because we have been told not to discuss these things, so some people may have trouble expressing themselves well. Be patient and helpful, for this will take some time.

- Do allow the facilitators to do their job; there will be times when it will not be easy. And remember, the facilitators and the members of your group are volunteers and nobody ever volunteers for an ass chewin'!

- Do use social media. You can open a Facebook account with the name based on a combination of your state, zip code or district number of your elected official. Twitter accounts can be named #JP<zip code>. Select an appropriate member in your group to manage the accounts for a period of time of maybe one year.

- Do try to be social. Make it a pot luck supper. You and some members may go to the bars or coffee shops afterwards—that's great. This makes it easier to communicate in the meetings.

- Do allow people who oppose your view to speak and finish their argument, and, do listen to their entire argument! It may change your mind after you hear the last words.

- Do watch out for people with hidden agendas, as they are everywhere, intentionally and unintentionally pushing their agendas or blocking progress.

- Do your research. Be able to back any statement you make. If you shoot from the hip and are proven wrong, people may never trust what you say again. Always make sure that your resources are correct and verified, rather than cutting corners and then having people believe that it is you who are wrong.

- Do go into this with an open mind. You may have gotten some bad information that has warped your thinking. It can happen to anybody. You may have heard a ten-minute news story that boils your blood, but missed the ten-second retraction a week later. It happens.
- Do allow your kids to come to the meetings and watch real politics in action. What a great impression this will make on them. Include your kids, especially teenagers, in their own jury system. Let them start calling some of the shots around town and in the operation of their schools—you may be shocked and amazed at what they come up with.
- Do allow certain people to be removed from future group proceedings if they are disrupting progress.
- Do be optimistic and determined, calm but tenacious. Voting for the lesser of two evils can no longer be an option because it always elects evil. Keep this in mind; we have no alternative but to take control ourselves.
- Do be patient. Your opposing view may be right, but the majority just may take a little more time to absorb it, even when presented with overwhelming evidence supporting your argument. You may lose the argument now, but with patience and good manners, you may win later. Realize that allowing everyone to express their views, listening attentively to them, and

then sincerely acknowledging what they've said, can reduce or dissolve a defensive reaction on their part and often enable them to relax enough to actually hear or accept another view.

The Don'ts

- Don't interrupt the proceedings with some personal agenda.
- Don't give up!
- Don't think for one minute that this will be easy—nothing worth accomplishing ever is.
- Don't sweat the small stuff. It's not about you.
- Don't let yourself think that you know everything and that everybody else is an idiot. You will not be of value to the group if you do. Remember, only you have walked in your shoes and there are good reasons others do not agree with you. Your views only fit your life—no one else's—so modifying your own idea to fit the group's thinking will become standard practice.
- Don't allow disruptive people to ruin the meeting and the group's progress.
- Don't allow people to make statements without supplying their sources. We want to trust the people of our group and be able to verify and confirm where they get their information from so the information or source is judged, not you. Eventually, a list of reliable news organizations may be created that the group can use as primary information sources. Also create a list of sources to be avoided—this will be very valuable and time-saving.

- Don't allow this new system to gravitate toward the existing political system or its methods. Some people may push for this simply because they are comfortable and familiar with the two parties. This is a jury-type party and therefore, random selection must be used or it will not be a jury type party.
- Don't create a hierarchy, meaning a situation in which the status or position of some members is thought to be higher than that of others. In other words, avoid a pecking order that entitles some people to be heard more often, or their arguments given more weight. If a new member comes to a meeting and listens to discussions, do not let them know who the jurors are right away because of special seating, badges or some other form of identification. Everyone in the meeting is giving testimony and discussing the issues on an equal level. It is only late in the meeting, if scheduled, that the jurors reveal themselves for the public vote. Only the facilitators should reveal themselves throughout a meeting. Openly resist any kind of hierarchy when suggested by a member or juror.
- Don't allow yourself to get emotional by losing your focus on good governance. Your ideas may not be supported or forwarded if you get too emotional.

So, are you interested in real "people power"? Then sign up at JURYPARTY.ORG and let's get to work on current issues and finding the next state or federal representative for your district. Who knows, it may be you!

Chapter 9 — The Opposition

You cannot escape the responsibility of tomorrow by evading it today. —*ABRAHAM LINCOLN*

The ultimate measure of a man is not where he stands in moments of comfort and convenience, but where he stands at times of challenge and controversy.
—*DR. MARTIN LUTHER KING*

It is the duty of the patriot to protect his country from its government —*THOMAS PAINE*

Power is going to defend you against the enemy. If you don't believe in the enemy then you don't believe in the power.
—*ARTHUR MILLER*

There will be great opposition to this movement, but on the other hand, there is a great defense of it as well. This movement will include Democrats, Republicans, independents and the disenfranchised—all who will come together as one voice. We won't agree on everything, of course, but we can be united because everyone has a voice that will be heard.

Let's look at each of the possible opposition groups and some ways the Jury Party can respond effectively.

The Media

The mainstream media is dominated by Democrat and Republican Party loyalists and controlled by the special interests that pay their bills and profit from government policy. If this movement gets on the media's radar, the media will oppose any alternative to the two-party system by using such catchphrases as: "threatening our way of life," "un-American," "undermining the system," "weakening America," "replacing experience with amateurs," "creating chaos,"—and let us not forget the Fox News classic, "Why do you hate America?"

Many of these assaults should be ignored, but if the opportunity arises, always respond by speaking of the success of bringing all people together in a common cause to find solutions to the nation's current problems. Also respond with statements such as these:

> "Why do you see the American people as threatening?"
>
> "This system is apolitical, that is, we do not have a philosophical platform as the other political parties do."
>
> "We open the door for all people to speak."
>
> "Our Founders understood the benefits of change."
>
> "We get the people involved in their community, state and nation."

> "You disagree because it greatly reduces the campaign spending that you have become accustomed to every two years,"

and so forth. Here's a good one:

> "If you do not trust the people to run the government, then how can you trust the people to select the right politicians to run the government?"

Also, keep in mind that the current jury system in the courts has clearly not kept up with the expansion of government. It needs to expand to meet the requirements for implementing the checks on *government abuses* that the jury system was created to do for the civil and criminal justice system eight centuries ago in England.

The media will fight against this because their very livelihood is at stake. Many of the special interest groups that influence our politicians also pay the media's bills. If we start winning elections then the money that the special interests give to the two parties will be wasted. The special interests will then give their marching orders to the media elite. It will be a substantial challenge. The media does not have to actually degrade the party with facts. The media only has to ask questions such as "Will the Jury Party change America?" or "Will the Jury Party replace the two-party system?" Scary questions such as these convince half the people that the answer is yes even if the answer is no. And they repeat these questions over and over at every commercial break in order to project negative feelings that will bias the viewer when the segment discussing the question airs.

Network pundits that spew out their radical liberal and conservative beliefs are not good for America and this system will shut them up by educating the pundit's audience, who will eventually abandon these extremists. Liberals, conservatives and moderates will find common ground (how else can you progress?) and that common ground is good governance. Slightly liberal leanings in some communities and slightly conservative views in others will occur depending on the character of the people who live there. Sharing each other's beliefs and concerns educates us in understanding where the other person is coming from; what, exactly, is driving their concerns? Here is a strong comeback from any criticism:

> "We are finding common ground, something that all people would like to see more of because the two main parties are incapable of doing so."

One argument against a jury system of representation might be lack of accountability. Since the system's representatives are rotated in and out of tier leadership roles, they are not accountable for their actions. But they will not be able to hide their mistakes either. In fact, there is little reason to hide mistakes since the decisions are made by honest individuals who are just trying to find an answer to a problem in a group setting. It will be unnecessary to form a witch hunt because of a bad decision—just fix it. In all likelihood the participants will be as much a victim of poor decisions as anybody else and simply report to their jury that the poor results were unexpected. Also, a decision with poor results will be quickly recognized and fixed because the next group, half of whom are selected within one year, does not have to defend the first group's position for fear of appearing incompetent. The system becomes self-correcting due to the fact that many solutions may require several try-and-fail attempts before a really workable solution is found. This system makes the process faster because you won't have politicians constantly defending their original solution, even though it has obviously failed. The Jury Party will no longer defeat proposals for improvements and change in order to protect their egos, their party reputation or their chances for reelection.

Another argument against juries will include the fact that juries have convicted innocent people and allowed the guilty to go free. True. But an investigation into these cases may discover another reason besides the human error factor. The information the jury receives is highly controlled. There are corrupt and incompetent district attorneys and police investigators, political pressure and biased judges. Information to free the innocent is held back, testimony to convict the guilty is declared inadmissible.

The jury does not make these mistakes. The systems that feed information to the jury make the mistakes. The jury described in this book is not controlled by anything but its own standards of proper behavior formed by the morals, ethics and values of its members—the American people.

Also keep in mind that a person in this system who winds up in Congress will have to spend at least six years discussing and proposing laws in direct contact with their peers in the Jury Party. They will have to gain the trust of many of the people they work with and be lucky enough to get through the random selection process. Additionally, they have to be selectable at the right moment when the incumbent resigns or is rejected. Anyone who has ambitions to be a political leader would be wasting their time going through this system—it's just too easy to get bypassed. And, if elected, that person has little freedom but to abide by the will of their constituents. What "entitled" person would settle for that? But while politically ambitious people will likely consider these barriers distasteful and choose not to persist in the Jury Party, those who do should be more interested in remaining accountable to the people while in office.

I have mentioned many times in this book that the people need to seek the truth and you may be wondering at this point how that can occur. First, the Jury Party will bring many people from many backgrounds into this organization who have specific, firsthand knowledge of events. They also bring in specific skills that can inform the group on current issues. And there are quite a few alternative media sources available, primarily through the internet, run by journalism professionals who have abandoned the mainstream media. These information sources can be invaluable for finding accurate and complete information to develop successful paths to alternative solutions and compromise. There seems to be a growing rebellion among journalists who discover that their chosen employer does not practice the art of journalism the way they believe it should be practiced. Search the internet for these sites to find the accurate and truthful information sources you need to make rational and practical decisions. The Jury Party may be able to create a media rating system that assists you in speeding up your searches for truthful information.

The mainstream media may not be as powerful as you might think and may be very vulnerable to a viable alternative. According to Nielson Media Research as reported by TVBYTHENUMBERS.ZAP2IT.COM during the week of March 25, 2014, the three major network evening news programs were viewed by a total of less than 25 million viewers. Cable news programs only reached about 2.65 million viewers on March 26, 2014 for a total share of less than 15% of the population. Over 85% of the people in America ignore these news programs or get their information from coworkers, friends, relatives or the internet. These 85% need a new source of information—a source that is complete, verified and truthful. The Jury Party can be that source. The Jury Party can rate news organizations based on their level of truth and most importantly, their level of completeness. A news organization may be truthful, but if they ignore the facts and evidence that diminish or disprove their biased beliefs, then they are not giving us the whole truth, and this can no longer be acceptable. And the party ratings of these news and information sources can be constantly reviewed and updated by the Jury Party members through Project Juries—this will be a major time saver for everyone.

I'll tell you one thing that will happen if this system gets national attention. You will definitely know who the elitists are. The elitists are those who refuse to accept the power of the country being in the hands of the people. So we will just have to prove our worthiness by electing representatives and developing solutions to problems through a political party that proves the American people are perfectly capable of running their state and country.

Before we leave this section I want to make a clarification. There is a difference between the mainstream media and the profession of journalism. My view of their differences is that they are totally unrelated to each other; the mainstream media is a business, journalism is a profession. One is after profits and the other is after the truth. The nine thousand member Society of Professional Journalists (SPJ), along with 38 other journalism and open government groups, wrote a letter to President Obama dated July 8, 2014, calling on the President to "stop the spin and let the sunshine in."[28] The letter begins "You recently expressed concern that frustration in the country is breeding cynicism about democratic government. You need look no further than your own administration for a major source of that frustration." Whoa! These journalists know how to get to the point fast. Sure don't see this kind of commentary from the White House Press Corps, do we?

The letter states "Over the past two decades, public agencies have increasingly prohibited staff from communicating with journalists unless they go through public affairs offices or through political appointees." The SPJ "considers these restrictions a form of censorship—an attempt to control what the public is allowed to see and hear."

This censorship is happening despite Obama's pledge on his first day in office to create "a new era of openness" in the federal government. The letter goes on to describe the various problems and barriers journalists have in communicating with government employees that have been implemented over the last two administrations (note: Republican and Democrat). And this, "A survey found 40 percent of public affairs officers admitted they blocked certain reporters because they did not like what they wrote."

Journalism ("the press") is the only profession mentioned in our Constitution whose rights and freedoms are guaranteed to keep the American people informed so they can make rational and intelligent decisions on Election Day. But if the government restricts access to that information, the American people are voting blind which will eventually result in a real threat to the people's constitutional rights. The letter adds "Meanwhile, agency personnel are free to speak to others—lobbyists, special-interest representatives, people with money—without these controls and without public oversight." The lesson here is do not confuse the media with journalism; seek authentic, professional journalism and avoid the mainstream media when possible.

The Two-Party-System

The two-party system has been around for a long time. But the two parties seem to have devolved into extreme points of view that few Americans believe entirely. They have become a two-dimensional system of conservative and liberal philosophies. But we live in a three-dimensional world of diverse opinion that requires far more options. No doubt the supporters of the two-party system will defend their beliefs adamantly. Both parties will do whatever they can to diffuse the Jury Party movement if it ever poses a threat to their system. They may devise alternatives that will placate the people while keeping their hold on the power and decision-making authority.

The special interests which control many of the policies of the two parties will do everything they can to discredit this system of selecting representatives. They will point out every single flaw in the Jury Party (or make something up) using their contacts in the media to spread their message.

It will be very important for every Jury Party group that is formed to be very protective of their image. Resist fights, diffuse hostility, and create an open forum where everything is on the table. Any one member of a group can be and should be removed if he or she is viewed as hostile toward anyone else. That behavior simply cannot be tolerated. Understanding, compromise, patience and cooperation are the golden rules of this system.

Registered Democrats and Republicans are more than welcome to join this system; in fact I strongly encourage it. It is my hope that they will abandon their two-party loyalty for an obviously superior system of selecting representatives which intimately involves the people in the decision-making process.

This may be viewed as a democracy versus a republic battle. If so, there are many one-liners that will be used against this democratic system by the two parties—for example, "A democracy is nothing more than mob rule." This statement is often attributed to Thomas Jefferson, but according to MONTICELLO.ORG, no written record of Jefferson saying this exists. Also, "Democracy is two wolves and a lamb deciding what is for lunch," attributed to Benjamin Franklin. Again, no record of Franklin saying this exists according to internet searches. My comeback to the last one is: "A two-party Republic is a hundred lambs voting on which wolf will have lunch." The intent of the Jury Party is to remove the "mob" argument and reduce the fears of the elites at being minimized by the dominance of the masses. The work of the Jury Party is to bring forth a highly organized political system for ensuring that policy has been thoroughly reviewed and analyzed as the best possible solution to problems that require government involvement.

I do not know what the right economic policy should be, nor do I know what the right balance between environmentalism and industry should be, nor do I know whether a judge should be kept or removed from his position or whether an amendment to my state's constitution should be passed—unless I spend vast amounts of time studying for each and every vote. So I do not want to vote for these policies or individuals by just guessing at the best outcome or taking the advice of an organization or advocate that advises people how to vote according to their political philosophy and hidden profit.

But what I *do* want is a balanced discussion of facts. The intent of the Jury Party is to remove the guesswork from the equation. That is the essence of the republican form of government—just guessing at the ballet box and calling it democracy. But the republican form of government is not democracy because it forces individuals to simply pick sides in a schoolyard fight without knowing what the fight is all about or who started it. Democracy is action, action from a trusted system occupied by informed citizens with a passion for the subject and a tenacity for the truth.

Our two parties are simply the liberal and conservative factions within the old Federalist Party—the very factions that Alexander Hamilton and James Madison predicted would *not* occur in a republican form of government when they wrote Federalist Papers 9 and 10 respectively. I think that the core beliefs of the two parties are very similar; they only differ in their public platforms that many people base their votes on. The actual operation of the government, or the core government duties, changes little between Republican and Democrat dominance. Publicly they are very different and promote clear conservative and liberal views resulting in about a 50/50 balance among the voters, as if by design.

If the Jury Party becomes a strong competitor against the established two parties, then it is possible that the Democratic and Republican parties may combine into one party, thereby in effect re-establishing the two-party system we have today. I would welcome this event because it would provide the American people with a clear pro-federal republican agenda and a clear pro-local democratic agenda (these terms being used as in republican and democratic forms of government). This development can only help to refine and perfect the Jury Party process and expose its possible faults—faults that could be overcome by constitutional amendments or modifications to its processes. This will ensure that the Jury Party truly abides by its "people power" mantra and remains open to modifying its methods.

So my warning is this: there will be many elitists who will condemn the Jury Party and begin the debate about republican vs. democratic forms of government all over again. They may even defend the power of the Presidency, clearly a monarchial bias. Elitists do not want a democracy simply because of their irrational fear that the majority will take their power and wealth away from them.

So far, the elitists are clearly winning the battle against the people in this country, but one day, when elitists' fears get the best of them, they may move this country to a more totalitarian form of government. I think the American people are smart enough to know that the elitists of this world are an important part of society and that robbing them of their contributions and wealth would be self-destructive, but the elitists have their fears and only effective involvement by the Jury Party, exercising true democracy over a long period of time in competition with a "republican government" party, can relieve these fears.

Tradition and Traditionalists

Traditionalists are people who have been lifelong Democrats or Republicans. They believe there should be an elite group of individuals which has authority over themselves—an authority that is superior to them which make the complicated decisions required for our community, state and country. Their beliefs have a two-thousand-year history that will be tough to crack.

Most people may fall into this category. This is a hard sell. The system described in this book is the start of a nationwide effort by the American people to control their nation and their future. This system of selection and vigilance over our representatives will be designed by the American people and for the American people.

The original Constitution was written by elitists. Somehow, they were given the selflessness and humble characteristics to write a Constitution with the Bill of Rights that guaranteed rights for all the people (well, almost all), which became a significant accomplishment compared to the monarchies and elitist parliaments that dominated Europe at the time. Now we have a better understanding of real freedom, the general population is far better educated and information is quickly available. All that is left to be attained is a willingness to exercise our right to make the rules.

Traditionalists may be the group of voters that bring up the democracy vs. republic debate and argue that the founders of our country did not believe that democracy was a viable form of government. Federalist Papers Nos. 9 (by Alexander Hamilton) and 10 (by James Madison) argued that the republican form of government prevented what they called factions. They failed to see that two opposing political philosophies would become the dominating political parties of today. Before and during the approval of the Constitution, there were already two factions arguing for different forms of government. This inspired the Anti-Federalists to push for the Bill of Rights to protect the people's rights from an elitist republican rule.

In a republican form of government, a grievance forwarded by the people requires elitist approval of the grievance for there to be a positive government response. If there is no response from the elitists, then the people are frustrated and disapprove of their government, which creates protest. A jury system of representation creates a path for answering and alleviating the grievances of the people without requiring the approval of the elitists or the protests from the people.

One argument that can be made by traditionalists is the way the Jury Party can fix a mistake. Mistakes by governments can fester for years or even decades before politicians are willing to admit a mistake was made and fix it. Since our groups have much more frequent rotation of their members, we can recognize and fix mistakes more quickly. The people will report to the representatives what the problems are and propose solutions that can be reviewed and decided on by the people and representatives working together.

If we keep bad representatives and bureaucrats in power through the existing system, problems will not be fixed. A jury system provides a better method of weeding out the bad officials who perform poorly before they reach a level of power that could do harm. Additionally, a jury system gives authority and power to the good officials who want to get things fixed.

Traditionalists argue that they do not want to waste their vote on a third-party candidate. But continuing to vote for people you do not approve of is clearly wasting your vote. Occasionally I will discuss politics with people and close with a comment like "both parties are the problem, we need a new political party." Lately, I've gotten a lot of positive responses from these kinds of comments. The traditionalists might be ready to abandon the two parties sooner than expected. If you know a person who is a party loyalist, ask them this question, "If your party is so great, then why does it get voted out of office?" After all, if it had all the right answers, it would dominate the elections.

Learn your arguments well against traditionalists because many will resist to the very end. But if most can be convinced, then the people have a real chance of controlling our representatives and government.

Fear of Change

We are all afraid or at least suspicious of change, and we should be. The Jury Party will not force anything on the American people. It is an institution that will gain the trust of the people because it gets results and should not be defensive of its errors. The results should allay any fears the American people have as the movement grows. As jury group members talk to their neighbors, coworkers, friends and family with growing knowledge and confidence about what they are doing and what has been accomplished, fear, suspicion and skepticism should mostly fade, and in its place will grow hope and passion for the community and country.

The Jury Party should grow on its own merits, not be forced down anyone's throat. And, being an open system, if people are suspicious, then they should come, observe, join and get involved. Being familiar with the system will alleviate the fears.

It is likely that the Jury Party will be successful in local communities before gaining statewide or national attention. This will give Jury Party advocates a list of success stories to sell to the American people. These success stories will convince a lot of people that this system needs to expand and be tested in the state or federal system.

Willingness to Get Involved

Are the American people willing to get involved in their community and country? Will the people put forth the effort needed to make the Jury Party work? Many Americans do get involved in politics, neighborhood groups, community activities, charities and elections. Consider the rapid rise of the Tea Party and Occupy America movements. If we are successful, it may be these people, looking for a more effective method to influence their government at all levels, who will join and pull other people, including their opponents, into the Jury Party movement.

The fact that the Jury Party has no philosophical attachment may attract a large following of those who are dismayed with the current political system and its biased and corrupt political parties. If people who have a gripe about their local government had someplace where they could be heard and where they could find others who agree with them or can help them polish their arguments, then the Jury Party has a good chance at success—especially if it is organized and led by people who know how to get results.

Those successes, and the ability to sell those successes, will attract many people to this system. If fully implemented, I'm guessing the Jury Party may require as many as ten million Americans, with over three million actually holding jury positions and twice that number in the audience who are also members of Project Juries or just people expressing their concerns and opinions. That's a lot of people, but it is actually close to only 5% of the able-bodied adult population. I think this is a reasonable number because 5% will greatly influence the votes of the American people if the Jury Party policies and recommendations are communicated effectively.

Special Interest Groups

Special interest groups are those groups who want something from the American people which enriches them using government and/or the media to accomplish their goals.

This is the biggest and most threatening opposition, by far. Special interests essentially run state and federal legislatures unless some issue sparks a torrent of opposition with the people. Under the existing system, laws are passed that are written by special interests. Your representative probably hasn't read most of the laws that he or she votes for or against. They mostly vote the party line and learn the party "one liners" to defend their decision—that may be all they have time to do. These laws have one purpose: to take money out of your pocket and place it into the pockets of the special interests which sponsor the bills and support sympathetic leaders from the two parties.

Philosophical special interests, such as environmental and human rights groups, have been out-spent by the moneyed special interests and do not seem to be as vocal or influential as they once were. These groups may also be some of the first to join this party in numbers in an effort to regain their influence. Many of these special interests will have to present strong evidence to justify their position or tone down their views to formulate a more mainstream approach so as to attract popularity with others in the group.

A furious response from the people may sideline a bill from time to time, but the special interests do not give up. These efforts are pushed by very well-paid, highly skilled individuals who probably don't even see what they are doing to America and its people. It's just business. If they fail this year, they will rewrite, resell and try again later. Battling these special interest groups requires tireless, monumental efforts that are difficult to organize and maintain. The special interests know they will win eventually. The Jury Party may very well be the "go to" organization that can quickly mobilize and maintain a barrier that the special interests may never break through.

Removing the special interests' money from our political system is one of the primary goals of this movement. And with perseverance and hard work, this movement can and will do just that.

This movement will not remove lobbyists altogether. I see nothing wrong with lobbyists; they are simply selling the point of view of their clients. I do see a problem with lobbyists and their clients donating vast sums of money to campaigns and political parties to buy influence. I do see a problem with all expense-paid junkets for the politicians and their families and staff. I do see a problem with tens of thousands of dollars paid to politicians as speakers' fees, which is just plain legal bribery. I do see a problem with the legal insider trading that is done by members of Congress and their staffs—legal in their world and illegal in ours. All of this must go. Lobbyists and their clients will have to sell their agenda *to the people*—a much more difficult effort, requiring truth and honesty. If a particular interest group is shown to be dishonest with the people, they may never regain the people's trust—and that will be far too high a price for most interest groups.

The Government Itself

The special interests groups and the two parties have many friends in high government positions who can put up roadblocks against this movement. Government workers will fear losing their jobs. Laws can be manipulated and created by the two parties and government agencies to cause frustration and delay progress. The government is their source of power and wealth and they and the top government bureaucrats (many of whom are former executives from those same special interests), will not give it up willingly. There is no telling if, or how much, the government will be used as the instrument of oppression against this movement. But if the government is used to its fullest capabilities, we are in for a real battle. There are many good people who work in the government and we will be very dependent on them to keep the bad guys in check.

We can battle the government for years and years and make little progress. The government monopolizes the ear of people who are not involved in organizations that offer alternative ideas, such as the Occupy movement and others, and can easily manipulate their opinions using the media to extol its proven method of repeating a lie loud enough and often enough so that it becomes the truth. The aristocracy directs the government, and the Jury Party movement threatens the very source of power and wealth of the aristocracy.

You

Yes, you. Maybe you haven't joined up at the website yet, or you haven't gone to a meeting. What are you waiting for? You read this book this far because you recognize a serious problem with your country. Now hop to it!

But maybe first you need to ask yourself if you are the kind of person to join the Jury Party. I think you are a potential member of the Jury Party if:

- You are one of the people concerned about this nation's future and lack confidence in its leadership.
- You are not a voter who votes a straight party ticket.
- You are a republican or democrat who is disturbed by the special interests controlling your party.

- You challenge or question authority.
- You are frustrated by the barriers set up by the authorities to prevent change.
- You have a yearning to know what is really going on but frustrated at not having the right resources and friends you can discuss your concerns with.
- You are disenfranchised from the status quo.
- You are a member or follower of a third party and wish to express your views to a wider audience.
- You feel the wrong people are getting elected and running the system.
- You want to get involved in your community and are discouraged by the philosophical constraints of those organizations that appeal to you.
- You are plagued by the bureaucracy of government and the constraints of the political process.

And I'll leave you with this metaphor. Imagine that you are the owner of a business that has been in your family for many generations, such as a family farm. You no longer work on the farm but hand over the control to some guy with a great resume. Then you go home and wait for the profits to come in. Some years go by and the profits have disappeared so you hire another person with a great resume to run the business. More years later the manager says you need to invest your savings back into the farm in order for the farm to operate, so you do it. And further years later, after many investments and still no profit, you hire another guy with a great resume to run the business, because you are hearing grumblings from your customers that the food from your farm is of a low quality. But the manager you hired assures you that it was just a fluke and if you invest more money it will never happen again. You come out of retirement and are working two jobs just to get by and support the family farm.

One day you decide you've had enough and go to the farm to see what is going on, but you are stopped at the gate by a security guard who doesn't let you in. After several unreturned messages to the manager, you write an email and get a form response back thanking you for your interest. You call many times and finally get his assistant who gives you a sympathetic ear and an earnest plea that things are going to get better now. You give up and decide to fire the manager, but he gets high-priced lawyers, paid for by your business, to block your action. Unfortunately, you do not have the funds to fight this effectively in court.

Let's summarize this analogy: you are the people, the farm is government, the manager is your elected official, the expected profits are your expectations of government, the funds to the business are taxes, the farm foods are the services provided by government, the security guard is the police, the court is the election and the high-priced lawyers comprise the campaign funding sufficient to stop a campaign by an honest opponent who could make a difference.

It's really simple. The people need to merge with the government effectively and take responsible charge of their affairs. A ***disgruntled absentee owner*** is who we are right now.

Chapter 10 — Conclusion

And you, chiefs and governors of the people! Before dragging the masses into the quarrels resulting from your diverse opinions, let the reasons for and against your views be given. Let us establish one solemn controversy, one public scrutiny of truth—not before the tribunal of a corruptible individual, or of a prejudiced party, but in the grand forum of mankind—guarded by all their information and all their interests. Let the natural sense of the whole human race be our arbiter and judge. —*C. F. VOLNEY: The Ruins, or, Meditation on the Revolutions of Empires and the Law of Nature*

The world is a dangerous place to live; not because of the people who are evil, but because of the people who don't do anything about it. —*ALBERT EINSTEIN*

Posterity! You will never know how much it cost the present generation to preserve your freedom! I hope you will make good use of it. If you do not, I shall repent in Heaven that I ever took half the pains to preserve it. —*JOHN ADAMS, 2nd President of the United States*

The modern jury system was institutionalized 800 years ago during the Magna Carta by English feudal barons who were being aggressively oppressed by King John of England.

Since those days, government has expanded relentlessly into almost every aspect of our lives outside of the justice system, but the jury's area of responsibility has remained unchanged in eight centuries. Adopted through English Common Law, the jury system is an integral part of the U.S. legal system and has proven itself worthy of its status. Dismissing the jury system for most Americans would be unthinkable. It may very well be the most trusted institution devised by man.

We can use the jury system to control the laws and regulations of the state. The state, controlled by an agenda-driven aristocracy, judged only by its fellow aristocrats, can become the people's enemy, realizing few or no consequences from a dependent and fearful populace.

The system proposed in this book may be described as a Highly Structured Participatory Democracy where the people vote for policy instead of leaders. The Jury Party will be entrusted with developing and refining the structure and decision-making methodology to become effective at solving problems and moving society forward quickly and efficiently. Once the Jury Party proves itself to the general population by getting party members elected into high office and successful ideas presented and implemented, the system can begin being put forth into the system of government with the primary goals of discovering the truth and setting policy.

The Greeks were the first to use random representation 2,500 years ago. This was their instinct. This was man's instinct. Their system had flaws, but it wasn't bad for a first try. Their system has inspired mankind ever since. The Greeks had inspired city-states around the Mediterranean Sea to adopt their form of democracy, but could not connect with each other and form larger systems that could challenge the empires that were developing. These empires were able to gain great strength and size that eventually overtook the city-state democracies. For over two thousand years the people have been under the authority of authoritarian type governments in which certain people are given (or have seized) great control and authority over the masses. Magna Carta and its descendant, the U.S. Constitution, were efforts to rein-in the excessive powers of authoritarian rule.

When our nation was formed, our Founders were exceptional people who rebelled against the family dynasties and religious institutions of Europe by adopting many of the "sacred texts" of history such as the Magna Carta. They were American aristocrats, not by European blood lines, but by performance and hard work, and for a few, responsible inheritance. They created a government that punched holes in the wall separating the people from the aristocracy. They did not eliminate the aristocracy; they just opened the door for anyone to earn their way in and made laws to keep these dynasties from coming back. It was revolutionary thinking at the time and they were wildly successful.

Today the people are far more educated than any generation before us. The internet has provided us with enormous sources of information that we can access quickly and efficiently—information that was totally unavailable just twenty years ago. The truth can be found when many people from all walks of life join together for discussions and verification of statements in a common cause. And with the truth comes the good governance that we desperately need.

Now it is time for "We the People" to take the next step and control the influence of the aristocrats/elites in government and other institutions in the country. The argument put forward in this book does not ask the government to give authority back to the people, but works with the existing system as a political party, a member of the political system. This way, the trust in the jury system can grow as the skills, knowledge and intuition of the people increase with experience. The system described herein will not overtake the current system of law until the majority of the people become active participants or passive supporters. Then the people will have the systems in place to rule their land effectively and defend their rights from those who wish to use the government's authority for their own profit.

A political party based on the jury system seems to me to be the best path for the people to use to play an active role in their government today. The party will be a place where complaints are heard and action is taken to force the government to answer those grievances. There may be no other way for the American people to act to take back their power, for the government—any government—will never willingly let go of its authority. When you vote for a representative, you are voting for a ruler.

Various wings of the political spectrum which seek to dominate the proceedings will find no haven in the Jury Party. They may seek to gain influence during certain events such as the introduction of a major piece of legislation. First, they would have to vastly dominate the majority of the membership, which is impossible in an open organization that allows all people to participate. Additionally, the other philosophies are free to join and challenge any undue influence a particular political philosophy may have. Also, the existing jurors were probably picked before the controversy erupted, so the invading philosophy must wait until the next selection cycle occurs to gain any influence. Bottom line, I think such groups will be wasting their time and will go elsewhere to mark their influence. This system, like the judicial jury system, is open to all people regardless of political leanings—it must be, for all people must have a say in all things government.

Why will a jury system of representation reveal the truth? Well, it probably won't all the time. Influential people will be influential and be hooked on a biased or bad idea sometimes. The people who are suspicious of a policy might be too ineffective with their arguments, just plain lazy, too busy to properly investigate a proposal, or just sidetracked on other issues. But this is OK, because when a bad decision is discovered and becomes obvious, the jury will recognize the problem quickly and begin discussions on the corrections required. The jury will determine the problems resulting from the law, discuss the corrections and direct their representatives accordingly. I believe that a major characteristic of this party is to recognize flaws in generally good legislation and be able to develop and recommend corrections. There is no effective method of doing this today, but the practice of constantly reviewing and modifying legislation should be a standard operating procedure of all jury groups.

I have proposed redefining the aristocracy as "people who get things done." For the people who get things done, the rewards are usually wealth, power and influence. For a society to succeed, it must free its aristocracy within the confines determined by the people. For any society to fail, all it has to do is blindly follow the aristocracy, or crush the existing aristocracy with another that may be just as oppressive, or restrict the aristocracy from pursuing its passions. The people must let the aristocracy pave the road forward, but the people must keep the aristocracy on the road, in the direction the people deem correct. Complacent societies, blindly following the established aristocracy, have allowed their leaders to run nations and cultures into the ground throughout history.

How many empires in history are still flourishing? None of them are, because empires almost always die horrible deaths—they expand beyond their capabilities and allow their infrastructure to degrade or resources to become scarce, or become riddled with corruption and resort to tyranny against their own citizens. In today's modern world, this could become extremely threatening to the progress of mankind. An unleashed aristocracy has its fingers on nuclear weapons, powerful armies, national infrastructure, all modern communications, national sovereignty, economic livelihood and energy, food and water resources. The people must exercise their right to rule their land to defend itself from these well-armed and wealthy powers.

Through the jury system, the people will have the ultimate authority in the nation, their state and their community. People of all walks of life, political leanings, socioeconomic backgrounds and education levels will cease to be manipulated viewers of the political process and become active participants in it. People will learn to get along and find common ground—we do this all the time in our everyday lives. Moderate to effective results from compromises between the extreme beliefs will be common so progress can go forward. Solutions to problems will be based on truthful information which has no ideology or special interest. The natural desire of people is to compromise and progress. After all, it is through their efforts that their children will have a chance to achieve the best life possible.

Initially, we must influence the elections of our representatives and petition local governments on the issues concerning the people. Then, when the representatives are on the side of the people, the jury system can be expanded to every agency in government. No longer will government agencies act like their own entities, devoid of reasonable oversight and bowing only to their special interests-connected managers.

In conclusion, the premise of this book can be summed up as simply a continuation and, it is to be hoped, the resolution of the 2,500 year old struggle (begun by the Greeks) between the elitists and the people. The elitists have clearly dominated the scene for the last 2,300 years, but now may be a good time to turn the tide on this situation. Not a time to overthrow, but a time to create a true and defendable balance of power.

A jury system changes everything in our culture. We will no longer fixate on our individual ability to excel in society to the exclusion of the needs and concerns of the bulk of the American people—although that characteristic will still be prevalent—it must, for it is part of human nature to want to excel and achieve highly in one's field of endeavor. However, the emphasis will shift to focus on contributions to our community, our nation and hopefully to mankind. Success for our society comes from millions of contributors, not hundreds of ambitious career-climbers. There will be no more anointed ones leading the masses. They will be replaced by millions of voluntary contributors dedicating their time to discovering and participating in their passions.

The goal of this book and party is to find the "sweet spot"—the balance of power between the elitists and the people. The goal is not to allow the elitists to force the people into servitude, nor is it to anger the people into storming the castle. The intent of a jury system of government is to provide a system that creates and maintains this balance of power and influence.

Due to the fate of Greek democracy, we must be cognizant of Empire (or "Superpower," as we refer to empire today). Empires create vast powers that the leaders will adamantly defend. We, as the human race, cannot allow empires to continue or be created under any circumstances, anywhere in the world—for the nature of empire is to dominate and suppress the human spirit. Empires create just too much power in too few hands. There are even local examples of empire, such as a "good ole boy" network that controls the economy of your small town or a criminal gang that controls the streets of your neighborhood. All these local empires should fade away as the Jury Party progresses.

If you still believe that the elite or the "best" should rule over the people, then I leave you with these two final questions. If the people are not qualified to rule their land, then what makes them qualified to appoint (elect) the rulers who do? And, how can competent leaders be created from an incompetent populace? The fundamental flaw of the theory of republican government is that for a nation or state to be successful, an incompetent populace must elect competent representatives. Republican government has performed well in the transition away from monarchies and powerful elitist parliaments in the last two centuries, but now we must embark on the next step.

We, the people, with the right system in place, can and will make significant change. And the people will be able to control that change and take responsible charge of their nation in a new American era. Man has developed bits and pieces of the system required for this effort throughout history. So let us, the people, take those pieces of discovery—democracy (developed to bring about freedom and justice), together with the institution of the jury (devised by a stubborn defiance of oppressive authority)—to the forefront of our government.

Jury Party Mission Statement

I will end this book with a proposed draft of the Jury Party mission statement:

> The mission of the Jury Party is to prove and help realize the viability of democracy; to develop the structure and organization of an energized political party that promotes and helps safeguard our democracy; to promote the principles and practice of "responsible charge"; to raise the people's consciousness about the influence of institutions and to develop the skills and knowledge that will enable the people to responsibly govern their community, state and nation.

☆☆☆

About the Author

S. Roy Johnson is an electrical engineer married with grown children. After years of following and trying to make sense of the American political system, he was driven to begin a six-year journey to find a better way for government to operate. He pursued this aim by first discovering the origins of democracy, then by exploring how to incorporate the original concepts of democracy into the current political system through a new political party.

Notes

[1] Jeffrey M. Jones, "In U.S., Perceived Need for Third Party Reaches New High," October 11, 2013 at www.gallup. com/poll/165392/ perceived-need-third-party-reaches-new-high-.aspx, accessed 9/2/2014.

[2] www.monbiot.com/2013/11/11/why-politics-fails/, accessed March 30, 2014.

[3] "Political parties in the United States," http://en.wikipedia.org/w/ index.php?title=Political_parties_in_the_ United_States&oldid= 593371866, accessed February 6, 2014.

[4] Jeffrey M. Jones, "Record-High 42% of Americans Identify as Independents," Gallup Politics, January 8, 2014, www.gallup.com/poll/166763/ record-high-americans-identify-independents.aspx, accessed March 30, 2014.

[5] electproject.org/2015g, accessed January 17, 2015.

[6] Wolf, Richard (December 22, 2011). "Voters leaving Republican, Democratic parties in droves". *USA Today.* Retrieved June 20, 2012.

[7] Lyn Carson and Brian Martin, *Random Selection in Politics,* Praeger Publishers (1999).

[8] John Burnheim, *Is Democracy Possible?,* University of California Press (1985).

[9] The Jefferson Center of Minneapolis, Minnesota, www.jefferson-center.org.

[10] See note 7.

[11] Frank Prochaska, "The American Monarchy," *History Today,* Volume 57, Issue 8, 2007.

[12]www.whitehouse.gov/sites/default/files/omb/budget/fy2015/ assets/hist.pdf, accessed March 30, 2014.

[13] Laurence J. Peter, Raymond Hull, *The Peter Principle,* William Morrow & Co. (1969).

[14] *Wikipedia,* "Oligarchy—Political Theory," http://en.wikipedia.

org/wiki/Oligarchy, accessed on March 30, 2014.

[15] See Note 13.

[16] Dorothy Gambrell, "The 113th Congress, by the Numbers," *Business Week* (January 10, 2013).

[17] *Citizens United v. Federal Election Commission,* No. 08-205, 558 U.S. 310 (2010); 130 S.Ct. 876.

[18] *McCutcheon v. Federal Election Commission,* 572 U.S. ___ (2014), www.supremecourt.gov/oinions/13pdf/12-536_e1pf.pdf, accessed March 24, 2015.

[19] See Note 17.

[20] www.supremecourt.gov/opinions/13pdf/12-536_elpf.pdf, accessed April 6, 2014.

[21] See Note 17.

[22] *The Guardian,* 12/4/13, www. theguardian.com/world/2013/dec/04/alec-freerider-homeowners-assault-clean-energy, accessed on 3/18/14).

[23] *Susan B. Anthony List, et al., v. Steven Driehaus et al;* No. 13-193, Supreme Court of the United States, decided June 16, 2014.

[24] www. aolnews.com/2011/01/14/opinion-who-are-the-constitutional-illiterates/, accessed on March 30, 2014.

[25] http://stanleymilgram.com/milgram.php.

[26] See Note 7.

[27] jefferson-center.org/

[28] www.spj.org/news.asp?ref=1253, accessed 7/29/14.

www.ingramcontent.com/pod-product-compliance
Lightning Source LLC
Chambersburg PA
CBHW050112280326
41933CB00010B/1069

* 9 7 8 0 6 9 2 4 2 3 7 1 4 *